COACHING IN THE FAMILY OWNED BUSINESS

The Professional Coaching Series

Series Editor: David A. Lane

Other titles in the Series

COACHING IN THE FAMILY OWNED BUSINESS

A Path to Growth

Edited by

Manfusa Shams and David A. Lane

KARNAC

First published in 2011 by
Karnac Books Ltd
118 Finchley Road, London NW3 5HT

British Library Cataloguing in Publication Data

A C.I.P. for this book is available from the British Library

ISBN: 978 1 85575 788 2

Edited, designed and produced by The Studio Publishing Services Ltd
www.publishingservicesuk.co.uk
e-mail: studio@publishingservicesuk.co.uk

Printed in Great Britain

www.karnacbooks.com

CONTENTS

ACKNOWLEDGEMENTS

We are grateful to our authors for giving their valuable contributions, and for making the effort to join us in advancing our scholarly endeavour to promote good practices for family business coaching in particular, and developing coaching psychology in general. Special thanks to Oliver Rathbone and Lucy Shirley of Karnac for providing support and extended co-operation in all stages of our manuscript preparation. Last but not least, we are grateful to receive unlimited support and encouragement from Professor Stephen Palmer to develop the book proposal.

Dr Manfusa Shams and Professor David A. Lane
Editors

*To my very special gifted children, Anik and Sakb,
without whom my life would not be complete, for bringing me
unlimited positive regard, warmth, thoughtful comments,
creativity, and fun throughout the period of completing
this book.*

*Dr Manfusa Shams
April 2011
UK*

ABOUT THE EDITORS AND CONTRIBUTORS

Lloyd Denton works in emerging market businesses specializing in leadership development. His coaching in family companies focuses on generational succession and the critical relationships between family and professional executives. For global corporations in many sectors, Lloyd coaches senior country and regional executives, executive teams, and succession candidates in the Middle East and Turkey. His approach to coaching integrates a variety of approaches around a central emphasis on evidence-based coaching for business leadership. Lloyd is a founding partner and board director at Praesta, a leading international coaching firm. He also coaches in conjunction with INSEAD's executive education programmes in Fontainebleau and Abu Dhabi and has taught MBA courses in Organizational Behaviour at Istanbul Bilgi University. Lloyd is a former vice president of the European Coaching and Mentoring Council. He resides in Istanbul and Dubai.

David A. Lane, PhD, CPsychol, FBPsS, FCIPD, is Director of the Professional Development Foundation and Visiting Professor, Middlesex University, and contributes to leading edge research in coaching as well as supervising leading coaches undertaking

Doctoral research. He was Chair of the British Psychological Society Register of Psychologists Specialising in Psychotherapy, and convened the Psychotherapy Group of the European Federation of Psychologists Associations. His work with the European Mentoring and Coaching Council has been concerned with codes of conduct and standards, and kite-marking of coach training. Working with the Worldwide Association of Business Coaches, he has researched and developed the standards for the Certified Master Business Coach award. He is a member of the steering group for the Global Convention on Coaching. His work recently led to the award for Distinguished Contribution to Professional Psychology from the British Psychological Society.

Dr Ho Law is a Registered Psychologist (Chartered & Occupational Psychologist), Chartered Scientist, a Fellow of the Royal Society of Medicine, an international practitioner in psychology, coaching, mentoring, and psychotherapy. Ho is a supervisor and an assessor for chartership in occupational psychology at the British Psychological Society (BPS). He is also an assessor in applied psychology for the Health Professions Council. He is a founder member and Chair (2010) for the BPS Special Group in Coaching Psychology. He has had over twenty-five years experience in providing advice and consultancy for diverse sectors. Ho is a Consulting Editor of *The Coaching Psychologist*, and *Coaching – An International Journal of Theory, Research and Practice*; and an editorial advisory board member for *Coaching at Work*. He has received numerous outstanding achievement awards, including the Local Promoters for Cultural Diversity Project (2003), the Positive Image (2004), and Management Essentials Participating Company (2005). He is the principal author of *The Psychology of Coaching, Mentoring & Learning* (Wiley, 2007). He is the founder director of Empsy® Ltd, the President of Empsy® Network for coaching, and a senior lecturer at University of East London, School of Psychology.

Elisabeth Legrain-Frémaux is an ICF certified professional executive coach, founder and director of Banksia Coaching International, and co-founder of ATOEM Consulting. After starting her engineering career in France and Germany, Elisabeth lived and worked for over twenty years in the Asia–Pacific area. Her responsibilities led her to facilitate collaboration between European and Asian teams. Inspired by her interaction with different traditional Asian cultures, she is fully convinced that the personality and emotions of each individual can be determinant and universal factors in company success. She specializes in leadership development in multi-national companies and has helped many directors to leverage their role and the teams' dynamics in the context of strong cultural changes for the benefits of the company's contribution to its ecosystem's progress.

Elspeth May was a Founding Partner of leading executive coaching firm, Praesta Partners. She is a highly experienced coach who gained accreditation as a Master Coach from Middlesex University in 2008. Prior to becoming a coach, she had a successful career in the accountancy profession, and was a partner in KPMG for ten years, specializing in personal tax and financial planning. She was a Fellow of the Institute of Chartered Accountants in England and Wales, holds an MBA, and is currently working on a Professional Doctorate about the evolution of coaching relationships over time. Throughout her career, she has worked with senior leaders in a variety of organizations, many of which have been family businesses. Her previous published work includes a chapter for *10 Things That Keep CEOs Awake: And How To Put Them to Bed* (Coffey, 2003, McGraw Hill).

Stephen Palmer, PhD, is Director of the Centre for Coaching, London, an Honorary Professor of Psychology at City University and Director of their Coaching Psychology Unit, a Visiting Professor at the Institute for Work Based Learning, and a Director of adSapiens, Gothenburg. He is an APECS Accredited Executive Coach and Supervisor, a Society for Coaching Psychology Accredited Coaching Psychologist, and IABMCP Diplomate in Professional Coaching. He is Honorary President of the Society for Coaching Psychology and was the first Honorary President of the Association for Coaching, and the first Chair of the British Psychological Society Special Group in Coaching Psychology. In his 2004 BBC 1 television series, *The Stress Test*, he demonstrated cognitive coaching. During 2010–2011 he was the Co-convenor of the International Steering Committee for the International Congress of Coaching Psychology events. He is the UK Coordinating Co-Editor of the International Coaching Psychology Review, Executive Editor of *Coaching: An International Journal of Theory, Research and Practice,* and Consultant Editor of *The Coaching Psychologist.* His publications include thirty-five books, such as *Dealing with People Problems at Work* (with Burton, 1996); *Achieving Excellence in Your Coaching Practice* (with McMahon & Wilding, 2005); *Handbook of Coaching Psychology* (with Whybrow, 2007); *The Coaching Relationship* (with McDowall, 2010); and *Developmental Coaching* (with Panchal, 2011). In 2008, the British Psychological Society, Special Group in Coaching Psychology gave him the Lifetime Achievement Award in Recognition of Distinguished Contribution to Coaching Psychology.

V. Ramakrishnan is the MD of Change Partnership Singapore, and has been a trained executive coach since 1999. He started in his family's manufacturing business after a Masters in Technology, has over twenty-five years of operational expertise in setting up, leading, and turning around companies in Asia, has lived and worked in Europe, and was the MD and CEO of an American company's Asian operations. He has developed a comprehensive framework integrating strategy, risk, performance, and leadership development; developed and tested over the years, it incorporates directorial effectiveness with managerial efficiency. The combination has delivered swift and consistent results for family owned, regional, and multi-national companies and government departments/functions. He has contributed chapters on directorial dashboards in *Thin On Top* (Nichols Brealey, 2003); on strategy in *Developing Strategic Thought* (Profile Books, 2003); and on performance governance in *Handbook On Emerging Issues In Corporate Governance* (World Scientific, 2011).

Manfusa Shams, CPsychol, CSci, AFBPsS, is Consulting Editor of *The Coaching Psychologist.* She is a Registered Chartered Psychologist, Chartered Scientist, and Associate Fellow of the British Psychological Society. She is former Deputy Chair for the British Psychological Society's committee for teaching of psychology to other professions, and a member of the BPS Special Group in Coaching Psychology. She is former Associate Editor of *The Psychologist,* Editor of the BPS psychology of women section newsletter, Book Review Editor of the BPS psychology of women section review, and a Guest Editor of the *Asian Journal of Social Psychology*. Among her major publications is a co-edited book on *Developments in Work and Organizational Psychology: Implications for International Business* (Elsevier, 2006), and two leading journals: *The Psychologist* (special issue, 2005), and *Asian Journal of Social Psychology* (special issue, 2005). She is a registered test reviewer at BPS Psychological Testing Centre, an experienced author, editor, supervisor, peer-reviewer, and group facilitator. She completed her PhD in Occupational Psychology from the Institute of Work Psychology, Sheffield University as a Commonwealth Scholar. She has teaching, consultancy, and research experience of almost twenty years. At present, she is teaching at the Open University in England.

Emma Wallace is a Chartered Occupational Psychologist, Chartered Scientist, and Associate Fellow of the British Psychological Society. She also holds a Certificate in Coaching, accredited by Middlesex University and recognized by the Association for Coaching. Emma has been offering business psychology services since 1994. She runs Business Psychology in Practice, a team of chartered psychologists, offering professional services in individual, team, and organizational development, selection, and assessment and coaching. With extensive experience in the law enforcement sector, she has published a number of works on the subject of selection and assessment, training, and ergonomics.

Helen Williams, CPsychol, MSc, BSc is a qualified occupational and coaching psychologist, specializing in solution focused and cognitive–behavioural coaching. Working independently and as an associate consultant at the Centre for Coaching, she is a member of several professional coaching bodies (AC, SCP, and SGCP). Prior experience includes ten years with SHL specializing in management and leadership development. Helen has co-authored several articles and book chapters, including "Managing across generations" (Green & Williams) in *Developmental Coaching* (Sheila Panchal & Stephen Palmer, Eds., 2010); "Cognitive behavioural coaching" (Williams, Palmer, & Edgerton) in *The Complete Handbook of Coaching Psychology* (Sage, 2010); and "Coaching in organizations" (Williams & Palmer) in *International Handbook of Work and Health Psychology* (3rd edn) (Cary Cooper, Ed., Wiley, 2009).

Hande Yasargil is the managing partner in Turkey for Praesta, a leading international coaching firm. Trained as a psychologist and family therapist, she has executive experience in the Human Resources profession and a ten-year track record in coaching senior leaders in one-to-one and group settings with a clinical approach. A renowned columnist and speaker on leadership issues in Turkey, she has coached at senior levels in many family businesses. After completing the Coaching and Consulting for Change programme, Hande became a certified coach in the INSEAD Global Leadership Center, working in executive education programmes at INSEAD's Fontainebleau and Abu Dhabi campuses. She has taught MBA courses in Organizational Behavior at Istanbul Bilgi University. Hande served as President of EMCC Turkey, EMCC's International Conference Chair, and as Vice Chairman of The Turkish Personnel Management Association.

The family firm: an underestimated powerhouse for growth

Family firms have long been a key part of the economy of many countries. In the UK, many of our leading companies started as family firms and others still have family members as part of their governance. They are an engine for entrepreneurial talent, a major source of employment, and have longer-time horizons than alternative forms of corporate ownership. Yet, they are seen as somehow less interesting than, say, the private equity sector, in spite of a significantly higher turnover than that sector. They are an unacknowledged powerhouse. While the literature on the family firm is vast and the literature on coaching in business rapidly growing, the issues facing those coaching within this sector have been largely unexplored.

The family firm has to succeed as a business, otherwise, like all enterprises, it fails. Yet, it also has to work for the family, and the dynamics between these needs is critical if we are to understand how to work with a family business and coach within it. Yes, as coaches we have to understand the context of the business, but also we need be able to work with the subtle interplay of factors and to be trusted by the family as much as by non-family members.

We have wanted to include a book on the family firm for some time. We have to thank Dr Manfusa Shams for her passion for this subject and commitment to bringing this enterprise to a conclusion. It was her continuing energy that ensured that this happened. My sincere thanks as Series Editor goes to her. I also must acknowledge the efforts of our contributors, working in many countries. They have been able to distil widely varying cultural insights and yet make their work in all its complexity both interesting and welcoming to our readers. I can attest to how many conversations took place with them and their always enthusiastic support for this project.

They were selected, based on many conversations, as leaders in the field of coaching, who commanded considerable respect from their peers but were deeply committed to working with family businesses. In my own work in this sector, I have been struck by the complexity of managing the family and the business. Our contributors negotiate this area with great delicacy.

In commissioning this book, we wanted to ensure that the contributions made were both scholarly and accessible. This is not an easy task, and we believe our contributors have succeeded in bringing together both their academic and practical experience. We wanted our readers to be left with a real understanding of what it is like to coach in a family business. The stories presented provide a vivid insight into the complexities of the task and also show the care that the contributors take in their work with clients. We also wanted to offer a contribution to the literature on the family firm, as well as to the literature on coaching. I believe that the senior editor, Dr Shams, has succeeded in that task.

The rationale for the Karnac Coaching series is to provide academically grounded but practical books that offer a key reference source for professionals in the field. In this case, we feel this contribution will have something useful to say to family businesses, business coaches, researchers and students in family business as well as coaching. We have provided a preface which covers much of the material I usually address in the foreword, so will not repeat this here.

However, the book, we believe, succeeds in fulfilling that rationale as well as making a unique contribution to the newly emerging literature in the field.

To our readers and the increasing number who follow each new offering and whose interests we take seriously, we recommend the latest edition to the Karnac Professional Coaching Series.

We really hope you enjoy the book.

Professor David A. Lane
Series Editor
Professional Development Foundation

PREFACE

Despite the voluminous literature, there is hardly any published work on major issues in group dynamics affecting family businesses, for example, interpersonal relationships between family members, leadership, communication styles, emotions, and values as translated into business language, family traditions and ethics. Each of these issues is crucial to the effective functions of a group. A family business is essentially representing functions of a group; hence, it is important to examine group dynamics within a family business to trace any specific interpersonal interaction between family members, and to extrapolate essential psychological issues influencing family members in a business partnership.

Coaching techniques tailored to meet the needs of family business are not yet fully developed, especially in the context of group dynamics, and with a focus on family systems and psychotherapeutic approach. Work from family systems theory has increasingly influenced coaching in organizations, as coaches recognize that the dynamics present in such groups reflect some of the dimensions of family group. Yet, the family business reflects both sets of dynamics, family and work group. The forms of questioning that have proved to be useful in family systems work can also offer a way of understanding the interactions with the family business. This book explores ideas from a range of theoretical approaches to family systems as they apply to the family business.

Major factors in group dynamics, such as group productivity, members' satisfaction, leadership influence, and groups' sustainable future are affecting families in a business relationship. The communication pattern between family members is likely to be influenced by family's values and ethics; emotions in communication and relationship types between family members can dictate family business governance and succession. Particularly, close family ties may bring emotional responses to a defined task, which may facilitate positive actions, or may provoke negative responses leading to a detrimental effect on the business output. Increasing attention is now being paid to emotional intelligence in a business setting, with a less focused attention on emotional intelligence in a family business context. Nonetheless, these issues are important to understand the interface between family and family business. In this context, underlying attitudes and motivations of family members may also serve as an impetus to successful family business. The leading editor's recent research with family business is supportive of such assertion. The psychological processes in attitude formation towards family business by the members, the use of family-orientated attitudes, and family values enhancement during business functions are worth considering when the psychology of family business and related coaching needs are discussed.

Embedded within this discussion is a group operating in a family business. Family business will perform well if there is a tailor-made in-house coaching training for all members, as well as opportunity for skill enhancement being offered. There has been a growing number of organizations offering training and coaching to family businesses. However, many of these coaching services fail to appreciate the importance of group dynamics in a family business context, specifically, delivering coaching skills around the areas of group composition, interpersonal relations, communication styles, leadership, attitudes and values, emotions and ethics.

A coaching approach to address these aspects of group dynamic may also consider relevant theoretical framework, such as family system and psychotherapeutic approaches to provide robustness in addressing the group dynamics in a family business context.

This book aims to showcase scholarly work from leading coaching psychologists with an expectation that each author will provide thoughtful analysis of group dynamics, family systems, and psychotherapeutic approaches to family business coaching. The book will, thus, provide both a theoretical groundwork and a practical application of group dynamic issues to family business coaching practices.

The rationale of the book is to provide a key reference book for family businesses, practitioners, business coaches, researchers, trainees, and the psychology profession in general. It is believed that it will serve as an essential compendium, and a useful foundation to understanding the group dynamics of a family business. It is also expected to provide practitioners' input in family business coaching practices, with specific reference to knowledge enhancement and developing innovative and reflective coaching practices appropriate to family businesses. The book is expected to present a new direction in partnership between family group dynamics and family business. Thus, the book has a far-reaching goal and can benefit academics, practitioners, and business organizations.

The aims of the book are:

- to present a scholarly contribution to family business coaching practice from group dynamic and family system perspectives;
- to highlight family members' interpersonal interactional pattern as determining factors for the sustainable growth and success of family businesses;
- to trace the theoretical underpinning of family functions in a business setting;
- to present thoughtful analyses of some major developments in research approach and techniques in family business coaching;
- to set examples of good practice in family business coaching and provide an overview of ethical practice for using group dynamic principles in family business coaching;
- to discuss the major needs of family members for the effective functioning of a family business from a coaching context.

Coaching psychology is developing fast, as such; it is not possible to capture all issues in one book. However, we have tried our best to accommodate selected major issues in coaching family businesses, with a particular focus on the family dynamics in business.

We have found that editing experience is a unique opportunity to learn, share, create ideas, thoughts, and experiences. The benefits of working with international authors are providing further insights into the subject area from a diverse perspective. More importantly, we have developed excellent partnerships with our authors, who are so responsive, encouraging, and engaging. We have also developed a good partnership with our publisher: we are encouraged by the publisher's timely responses and impressed with their excellent service. These have, no doubt, helped us to complete the book.

Editing a book requires tireless effort and high commitment, and it is not possible to cover all the issues in a limited space. However, our authors have worked very hard to present their coaching experiences in the light of the family dynamics in a business context, and this dedication in writing is reflected in each chapter. We are particularly grateful to our international authors, who have put extra effort and energy into presenting their chapters in a language other than their own spoken language, without affecting the quality of writing in presenting the essential issues capturing the main theme.

The success of the book remains in the actual application of ideas and thoughts presented in each chapter to coaching practices.

Dr Manfusa Shams and Professor David A. Lane

Introduction

Manfusa Shams and David A. Lane

The emerging issues from coaching psychology and coaching experiences should be delivered appropriately to the businesses and academic world. From a family business coaching perspective, there is a pressing need to highlight the importance and usefulness of understanding major issues facing family businesses, and to apply appropriate coaching techniques to address these issues.

This book is expected to serve the need to develop a solid and sound foundation for innovative and appropriate family business coaching practices with a focus on current issues influencing family business, and to advance our knowledge about family business coaching from an international coaching context.

There has been a growing number of organizations offering training and coaching to family businesses. However, many of these coaching services fail to appreciate the importance of group dynamics in a family business coaching practice, specifically, delivering coaching skills around the areas of interpersonal relations, communication styles, leadership, values, emotions, and good ethical practice in family business. Family is central to family business coaching, as such we need to look into family dynamics and family functions to ensure an effective coaching practice to apply to family businesses.

Coaching has been used in sports and art industries for more than a decade; however, the usefulness of coaching to human development from a psychological perspective is relatively new. Interestingly, it is not known to what extent coaching has transformed an individual to achieve his or her full human potential, although coaching has been used to achieve success in sports and arts. Coaching psychology has come forward to map the psychological growth of individuals as a result of coaching. Coaching in the family-owned business has dual tasks for ensuring two types of growth: (a) family members' growth in understanding and maintaining effective interpersonal relations and communication, and (b) business growth arising from family members' growing commitment and shared concerns to reach business goals.

We are aiming to present scholarly contributions to address major issues in family business coaching practices, to highlight the importance of understanding interpersonal interaction in a family business coaching context, and to explore areas affecting the sustainable growth and success of family businesses from a coaching context. Furthermore, we aim to trace the theoretical underpinnings of family business functions for the delivery of an effective coaching technique, and to present thoughtful analyses of some major developments in research approach and techniques in family business coaching. The primary aim is to set examples of good practice in family business coaching, provide an overview of ethically sound family business coaching techniques from a practitioner's standpoint, and to discuss the major needs of family business coaching from international and cross-cultural perspectives

This book aims to showcase scholarly work from leading coaches and practitioners with an expectation that each author will provide a thoughtful analysis of good practice in family business coaching, taking into account major issues affecting family dynamics, business functions, sustainability, and progress.

The content of this book is enriched with practitioners' reflective experiential accounts, showcasing case studies from coaching practices and evaluation of authors' coaching experiences to ensure further refinement in coaching practice, with a focus on further development in coaching techniques for family business. Thus, the book has the far-reaching goal of presenting practitioners' standpoints to enhance good coaching practice in family businesses, and to present the delicate issues in coaching family members within the business context.

The distinctive feature of this book is that it presents authoritative contributions from experienced family business coaches who not only own and govern their own family businesses, but also work as coaches for their own and other family businesses, both locally and at an international level. These contributions represent valuable insights from a "home-grown" coaching perspective. The concept "home-grown" is used to refer to "self-coaching" for a family business by the family business owners. The deep insights drawn from "home-grown" coaching experiences will be a very useful foundation for developing family business coaching with an aim of exploring different coaching techniques for family business. We are indeed very grateful to these coaches for giving their valuable time and effort to distil their experienced views into words, with a shared vision of developing good and ethically sound family business coaching practices. Especially, the arguments for "family business owner driven coaching" are presenting new directions in coaching family business, and the possibility of practising the proposed coaching techniques both for local and international family businesses.

The book also presents scholarly work from leading coaching psychologists; these are mainly focused on providing an overview of coaching practices in the UK to date, the position of family business coaching within the coaching psychology, good ethical practice in family business coaching, the influence of family dynamics in family business coaching, innovative and solution-focused coaching for family businesses, and future directions. The book is, thus, unique in showcasing contributions from family business owners and coaches, along with coaching psychologists' thoughtful analysis of effective coaching practices and approaches to coaching family businesses. The collection in the book is a blended, solution-focused intellectual property in the market for family business coaching.

The book offers narrative accounts from business owners and coaches with the help of real-life case studies, and in-depth personalized and reflective discussion on promoting good practices to coach family businesses. The chapters from leading coaching psychologists present advanced, thoughtful analysis of selected techniques and approaches in family business coaching, with appropriate examples to illustrate major viewpoints. The contributions are expected to advance the scholarly movement to appreciate and recognize a new era for coaching with a psychological perspective.

The common thread running through all chapters is the influence of family dynamics in family businesses. The discussion in each chapter looks into major areas of family dynamics to explicate the complexities around family business, which are caused by both family dynamics and business functions. The aim is to highlight the importance of family dynamics in family business coaching so that equal attention and importance is given to coaching both the family and the family owned business.

Drawing on experiential accounts of coaching family businesses from selected leading coaches and practitioners, a realistic, critical, and reflective approach is taken to present each chapter in very simple, easy to access, and engaging language. The chapters are presented in a logical sequence to ensure continuity in presenting scholarly views, and thus the smooth progression from one chapter to the next is ensured.

The chapters are presented in two parts. Part I (Chapters One, Two, Three, and Four) is dedicated to setting the groundwork for discussing family business coaching, and the second section (Chapters Five, Six, Seven and Eight) is exemplified with real-life case studies in family business coaching by the family business coaches, with a focus on narrative approach.

This Introduction presents an evaluation of the recent developments in family business coaching, with a particular focus on developmental issues pertaining to coaching psychology. It traces the development, institutional movement, research initiatives, local and international work in coaching psychology, the interdisciplinary contributions, the identification of coaching needs, and innovative coaching practices in the quest to map the boundaries of family business coaching. An integrative model incorporating all the essential steps in a good and ethically sound family business is offered in this chapter.

The critical discussion about finding an answer to the key question, "What is family business coaching?", is augmented by the evaluation of existing literature defining coaching and family business coaching in Chapter One (Shams). This chapter sets out to provide the foundations for family business coaching, which must give appropriate attention to the issues relating to the interface between family and business coaching, family dynamics, and the distinctiveness as well as inclusive features of family business coaching. The chapter concludes with an emphasis on family dynamics in family business, suggesting a dual-coaching practice should be in place: for example, coaching families to address any interpersonal and communication issues, and coaching family business in which business functions and goal attainments are the primary focus.

The fundamental question of defining the coaching concept has been eloquently discussed in Chapter Two (Shams). This chapter is a key section in this book, because the author endeavours to trace the development of coaching in psychological practice and how coaching psychology is emerging from existing coaching practices in various fields other than psychology. The extended discussion shows the way coaching has been implemented in psychology, especially for business, thereby linking it to family business coaching. The arguments for a business coaching specific to a family context are supported by two case studies, and the need to trace the key issues for family business coaching in both local and international contexts is highlighted. The chapter also includes the scale of the contribution of family businesses to the national economy of different countries, and major factors affecting the size and extent of economic contributions from family businesses.

The powerful discussion in Chapter Three (Williams, Palmer, and Wallace) includes an evaluative perspective on the application of an integrative coaching approach to unlock human potentials within a specific context, such as a family business. The challenging issues in coaching individuals with apparent psychological blocks / restrictions are addressed with the use of three prospective models. The chapter offers an engaging, credible, and effective mechanism for coaching conversation with family businesses, and the justified positions and invaluable contributions to coaching family businesses using three models—PRACTICE, Stress Mapping, and ABCDEF.

In Chapter Four (Law), ethical and culturally appropriate coaching practice for family businesses around the world is presented, using a narrative coaching approach and six ethical principles. The chapter adds novel insights into the way our knowledge about family business can be enhanced with a good understanding of the universal integrative framework in coaching across cultures, and the practical value inherent in this framework in the context of family business coaching. The chapter ends with a scholarly discussion on family business coaching, and the potential for advancing coaching psychology further with the selected models, key techniques, and identified key issues.

The issues of family dynamics have been looked in depth in Chapter Five (May) with the help of two case studies drawn from the author's own coaching practice. The author advocates very clearly the message about the complexity around family businesses, and the way a family business is influenced by family dynamics, hence any coaching practice for a family business must incorporate family relations, communications, emotional issues, and values. This chapter, together with the previous three chapters, provides significant insights into the key role a family plays in shaping a business for sustainable development.

An insider's perspective, with powerful reflective analysis from extensive coaching experiences, is presented in Chapter Six (Yasargil and Denton). The chapter offers excellent cases from the authors' coaching experiences, and uses engaging language to unpack the complexities in family relations that affect family businesses. The chapter draws deep, thoughtful examples from selected family businesses to show the emergence of two types of coaching approach, one "family first" and the other "business first". The critical discussion is exemplified with appropriate cases. The authors argue that coaching techniques for family businesses are drawn from family psychotherapy, psychoanalysis, family systems, and organizational behaviour areas, without the clinical properties in each approach, hence family business coaching is built on approaches and techniques shared by other disciplines.

Chapter Seven (Legrain-Frémaux) presents an unexplored and interesting area in coaching with expatriate family businesses. The chapter introduces the author's narrative account and personalized discussion on major issues in coaching expatriate family businesses with the help of few selected case studies. The chapter draws the reader's attention to the prospective development of coaching in this unexplored area, and the way family dynamics can build up the bond between families and their businesses.

The personalized and narrative discussion on coaching family business with a focus of family dynamics has been augmented in Chapter Eight (Ramakrishnan). The chapter bridges the gap between the essential issues in family functions and business functions in a family context using sensitive and appropriate examples and case studies. The author has invested his coaching experiences to draw relevant issues for the further development of coaching practices in family business, for example, concepts such as family constitution and organic renewal.

The last chapter (Chapter Nine, Shams) summarizes the key issues discussed in each chapter for the development of appropriate, ethically sound, and culturally appropriate coaching techniques for coaching family businesses. The discussion is presented with the help of few diagrams to frame the authors' leading ideas and thoughts, so that further work can be done to popularize family business coaching using solid theoretical groundwork and specific practical tools. The discussion ends with the reaffirmation of the central role of family dynamics in a family business. Suggestions of practical steps to untangle the complex issues around coaching practices for family business are an added attraction to this chapter.

Conclusion

This book intends to open up the process of compiling coaching experiences for the development of coaching techniques and approaches for family businesses. Most of our international coaches do not have extensive experience in presenting their views formally in writing, and this may have reflected on their expressions in writing. However, we believe the messages delivered are clear, informative, and very valuable, as they come directly from family business coaches with experience and coaching skills, both as family business owners and coaches. This book makes an exception to present these unexplored areas: what is the difference between coaching practices by the family business owner and coaches without any ownership of a family business? How do we justify the need for coaching families independently of family business coaching? How might we use transferable coaching skills in the context of family business?

The book generates interest in documenting coaching practices for family businesses, and as such it is the beginning of a journey to show the growth of coaching rather than the end, albeit depicting family business coaching through active theorizing, consultations, and practical interventions for minimizing the gap between a family and their business.

CHAPTER ONE

Key issues in family business coaching

Manfusa Shams

Introduction

Coaching as a practice is a vibrant area, developing continuously with the demands from different disciplines. One such new development is "coaching psychology", and the gradual emergence of family business coaching embedded within coaching psychology. This area is still too immature to suggest any definite framework upon which family business coaching is built. However, we were able to gather together existing practices in order to present key issues based on these cumulative coaching practices for family businesses. One of the fundamental issues is whether the concept "coaching" can be applied universally to all coaching practices. To answer this question, we have to look into the meaning of coaching. The following sections will make an attempt to find the existing definitions of coaching, main features, and, finally, the definition of family business coaching.

What is coaching?

The best way to answer this is to get an overview of the existing definitions and then extrapolate key terms from the existing definitions of coaching. The focus of this book is coaching psychology, hence only a few recent simple and complex definitions of coaching will be presented, followed by an evaluation of each definition to suggest common key features and the underlying meaning of the definition provided for coaching.

To start with a simple definition, "coaching is the art of facilitating the performance, learning and development of another" (Downey, 1999). An extended definition is by Grant and Stober (2006):

> coaching is a collaborative and egalitarian relationship between a coach, who is not necessarily a domain-specific specialist, and coachee, which involves a systematic process that focuses on collaborative goal setting to construct solutions and employ goal attainment process with the aim of fostering the on-going self-directed learning and personal growth of the coachee. [pp. 1–14]

A simple definition from an interpersonal relationship context is "a systematic procedure enacted within a helping relationship that has the aim of fostering the coachee's development" (Stewart, Palmer, Wilkin, & Kerrin, 2008). Another definition takes a social constructionist perspective to define coaching, for example, "coaches participation in the development and learning process of the person in focus. This process creates the foundation for new, alternative, or revised narratives of the focus person's personal and professional life" (Stelter, 2007). A more formal definition of coaching is offered by Grant and Greene (2001), "coaching is a solution-focused, result-oriented systematic process in which the coach facilitates the enhancement of work performance and the self-directed learning and personal growth of coachee", which has been analysed by Senior (2007), "coaching is revealing itself as a unique system of communication that seems to facilitate excellence in performance and enhance quality of life across work and home domains". Yet another recent definition has given emphasis to the therapeutic parts in coaching practice, "coaching psychology is for enhancing performance in work and personal life domains with normal, non-clinical populations, underpinned by models of coaching grounded in established therapeutic approaches" (Grant & Palmer, 2002).

An in-depth review of these definitions shows the following major features of coaching concept:

- maximizing human potential;
- personal growth and self-directed learning;
- solution-focused and performance enhancement;
- facilitator for goal-attainment.

Now the question is, where does psychology fit into this picture of coaching? Obviously, this question was the main driving force behind the development of coaching psychology in the UK. Psychology deals principally with behaviour, hence coaching psychology deals with human behaviour to develop and nurture human potential to a maximum level. Coaching psychology incorporates all types of coaching, for example, life coaching, executive coaching, business coaching. Therefore, family business coaching is one such coaching practice, embedded within business coaching.

Major features

Recent attempts to conceptualize coaching from an applied psychological perspective are focusing on the functional elements of coaching. Various dynamic concepts, such as "stages", "personal creation and recreation for meaning in experiences gained" and "pathway to growth" (Lane & Corrie, 2009; Stelter, 2009) are used in the ongoing discussion on coaching.

There is a growing interest to ground the concept "coaching" in various theoretical frameworks so that appropriate techniques can be applied in coaching practice. However, this is still at an experimental stage, remains to be unfolded to appreciate the need for a solid theoretical grounding for coaching psychology. The delay in defining coaching psychology is due to continuous negotiation over varying issues in order to settle the dispute over ownership of the coaching concept, as it was very much a monopoly of sports (Stelter, 2009), so the question remains: how do we accept a general coaching concept, applicable to all disciplines, thereby ensuring generic coaching skills, which can be blended into coaching practice for diverse disciplines?

What is family business coaching?

Typically, a family business refers to a business owned by family members, which may or may not be founded by a family member (Shams & Bjornberg, 2006).

Family business coaching shares the central tenets of business coaching, but, in addition, it is directed to coaching a family as a social unit independent of business functions. Therefore, it also embraces the essential coaching technique for families, and presents a dynamic and distinctive feature for this type of coaching.

Key issues in family business coaching

The major emerging issue in family business coaching is the presence of a blended coaching approach for family businesses, with an interdisciplinary focus in practice, in which fusion of counselling, psychotherapy, and psychometrics is evident. The blended coaching approach highlights the importance of family in business coaching, hence, family business coaching can be characterized by coaching for the family by the family business owners and coaches, implying that coaching is provided by many family members themselves when they grow and gain longstanding experience in various business sectors. This is verified by some of our authors, who are owners of family businesses as well as working as coaches both for their own businesses and for other family businesses.

There are common issues running across all types of coaching, for example, application of active listening, empathy, non-judgemental attitudes, openness, and transparency. However, there are distinct issues in family business coaching, related to family functioning and family therapy. Counselling also plays a major role in family business coaching. The focus is on the family by the family business owner in the interests of developing a sustainable business; hence, issues originating from a family context must be addressed in coaching sessions. Any coaching intervention is based on a two-tier system—family intervention and business intervention.

Family dynamics in family business coaching

The major areas in family dynamics are family types, relationship patterns, and communication styles between family members, and nature of holdings and position in the family business. A case study (Shams, 2006) is presented here as an example of the presence of family dynamics in family business coaching:

Case study A

Two brothers are founders of a family business, which was later further developed by one of the brothers' wife. The other brother's wife is not active in the family business with no ownership, executive, or governance responsibilities. The eldest brother has two sons, only one of whom is involved in the family business, performing executive and governance roles. None of the second brother's three children are interested in the family business—they are neither involved in the family business nor have they been assigned any executive or governance roles as successors. The structure of this family business suggests a complex family dynamic in which the elder brother's family has more involvement than the younger brother. This may indicate that the elder brother has a dominant influence in running the family business, raising the question of how the business functions, and how decisions are being made with the younger brother, who does not have anyone from his family to actively contribute and support him in family business functions.

Interface between family and business

In a family business, family and business are not opposed to each other; rather, it is a blended functional product, where a family turns to the business to meet economic needs. As such, families and businesses are working in partnership to generate economic function and sustainable growth. The transaction between a family and a business is enhanced and facilitated by that family's distinctive features, such as family structure, number of family members involved in the business, their positions, and communication and relationship patterns. A typical picture is presented below (Shams, 2006).

Case study B

A family business is being operated by a family member (nephew) other than the founders' children due to the lack of interests and apathy to get involved in the family business. The nephew has taken on a main executive role, making him the obvious choice to run the business upon the death of the founder, thus raising the issue of succession in a family business where a relative has more ownership and executive role than the founder's children!

Family business coaching in the business world

The business world is vibrant; therefore, family business coaching must find the most appropriate course to establish its position. The legitimate position of family business coaching depends on the successful application of various coaching techniques to the development and progression of family businesses. Ironically, despite the high percentage (Shams & Bjornberg, 2006) of family businesses among all businesses in the world, there is still a lack of consolidated literature on family business coaching practices, which may well be because family business coaching has been taken for granted and the need to develop a solid theoretical base with practical applications, on which family business coaching can be grounded, has not been sufficiently appreciated. This may also be because coaching has been carried out following a business transaction model, without necessarily valuing the inherent potential of the coaching practice to influence and enrich the family tapestry in relation to business. It would also be worth exploring the views of family members in business, and their attitudes towards family business coaching, so that the effectiveness of family business coaching can be documented and future directions in family business coaching can be offered from a family *vs.* business perspective.

Family business and economy

The complexity involving family business functions and diversity in management and operational style does not lessen the significant contribution of family businesses to the national economy. Recent literature (Duh, Tominc, & Rebernik, 2009) suggests that, in the USA, family businesses currently account for eighty per cent of business organizations, produce over fifty per cent of the gross national product (GNP), and employ more than fifty per cent of the domestic workforce (McCann, DeMoss, Dascher, & Barnett, 2003). In several European countries, family businesses represent the majority of all national economic output, for example, France 60%, Germany 60%, and in the UK 70% (IFERA, 2003). There has been discussion in the literature about various factors affecting the nature and size of economic contributions from family businesses to the national economy.

These are:

1. Family business size: Westhead and Cowling (1998) have demonstrated that family businesses were generally smaller in employment as well as sales revenues than were non-family enterprises. This is evident in other European countries as well, for example, according to Vadnjal's (2005) conservative (bottom-line) estimation; family businesses contribute only twenty-two per cent to the total added value of the Slovenian economy.
2. External market: Family businesses tend to be locally based; as such, they are far behind the non-family businesses in terms of international sales levels, hence economic contribution is minimal.
3. Personal agency: Family involvement in a business can both increase and decrease financial performance due to agency costs (Chrisman, Chua, & Litz, 2004). Agency theory is employed to explore the relationship between a firm's ownership and management structure and its financial performance. Where there is separation of ownership and control, agency control mechanisms are put in place to align the goals of managers with those of owners.
4. Primary focus: In a family business, the main focus rests on non-financial objectives, such as family functioning in a business

context. However, this can have an adverse effect on the economic contribution of a family business (Westhead & Howorth, 2006).

5. Productivity rate and economic growth: If the family business is part of a small business, then contributions to the economy can be two-fold: changing market economy through the renewal process, coupled with the fact that this type of business may encourage growth in the labour force, particularly among the unemployed.

6. Economic growth via intergenerational transmission: Family businesses can ensure continuing economic growth through generational transmission in economic activities, without any gap in economic transfer and with low risk of unemployment even when productivity is at a low level or has declined due to economic interdependence, thus ensuring productivity and growth (Robbins, Pantuosco, Parker, & Fuller, 2001).

Family businesses are increasingly playing a major role in the national economy (Mandl, 2008; Duh & Tominc, 2006). If family businesses represent 70% of all businesses in the UK, obviously family businesses are contributing significantly to national economic growth. However, the various contribution percentages, in terms of performance, growth, and financial output, still need to be ascertained.

Localized and global family business coaching

Coaching practice is influenced by local context and local knowledge is a driving force in facilitating good coaching practice (Shams, 2006). Global coaching, however, can serve both local and global coaching needs. For example, global coaching techniques can be adapted to a local context to benefit local businesses. All business coaching is tailored to meet the needs of businesses seeking coaching; hence, coaches have the power to choose and manipulate coaching practices to suit local demand. This can be a developing issue, as new ideas and thoughts may arise from localized coaching practices, which can then be applied at a global level to explore the feasibility of the practice in a wider context. Another issue in this context is coaching practices owned by coaches, which may never have been shared with others, thus these practices remain private affairs for the coaches, accessible only to them, with no external feedback and reactions to assess the effectiveness of these localized coaching practices. This practice may be the result of a lack of any regulation or regulatory framework to monitor various coaching practices relating to family businesses, largely due to the private nature of such businesses, and of idiosyncratic coaching practices run by independent coaches as part of their private organizational functions. Our authors in the second part of this book, who are family business owners and coaches, present further discussion on this issue.

Crafting family business coaching

Coaching practice in family businesses has distinct features because coaching practice is designed to include specific features of a functional family, such as, family values, ethics, traditions, interpersonal relations, emotions, communication patterns, and leadership style. No other coaching type has such a diverse range of issues to deal with in a coaching intervention. The task of family business coaching thus requires delicate crafting to ensure that each part of the family tapestry is being given appropriate attention and suitably integrated into the overall design of the coaching intervention. The speciality of family business coaching is, therefore, not focused only on family issues, but also on the interface between family and business, so that the coaching intervention takes into account all major issues encompassing a family and their business.

Conclusion

Family business coaching has a long route with many diversions to arrive at an effective and ethical coaching practice. The diversions have emerged from different coaching practices in family businesses, and are influenced by different family and business types. However, the underpinning issue in family business coaching is family dynamics, and, as such, the development and formulation of family business coaching practice must incorporate all essential issues in family relations and business practices, both in a local and in a global context. The intertwined effect of family and business generates a fertile ground on which appropriate and ethically sound coaching practices for family business can be built and, therefore, increasing attention should be focused on the development of generic and specific family business coaching skills for sustainable growth of families, family businesses, and family business coaching practices. A collective effort from academics, practitioners, coaches, and businesses can ensure continuity in delivering good coaching practice for family businesses, along with a vision to promote coaching psychology around the world. This chapter has presented some of the key issues with the aim of developing these further to enhance good family business coaching.

References

Chrisman, J. J., Chua, J. H., & Litz, R. A. (2004). Comparing the agency costs of family and non-family firms: conceptual issues and exploratory evidence. *Entrepreneurship Theory and Practice, 28*(4): 335–354.

Downey, M. (1999). *Effective Coaching.* London: Orion Business Books.

Duh, M., & Tominc, P. (2006). Comparative analysis of family and non-family businesses in Slovenia (Primerjalna analyze družinskih in nedružinskih podjetij v Sloveniji). In: M. Rebernik, P. Tominc, M. Duh, M. Rus, K. Pušnik, T. Krošlin, B. Bradča & D. Močnik (Eds.), *Slovenian Entrepreneurship Observatory 2005 (Slovenski podjetniški observatorij 2005).* Maribor: Faculty of Economics and Business.

Duh, M., Tominc, P., & Rebernik, M. (2009). The importance of family enterprises in transition economies. *Eastern European Economics, 47*(6): 22–42.

Grant, A., & Stober, D. (2006). Introduction. In: D. Stober & A. Grant (Eds.), *Evidence-based Coaching: Putting Best Practices to Work for Your Clients* (pp. 1–14). NJ: Wiley and Sons.

Grant, A. M., & Greene, J. (2001). *Coach Yourself: Make Real Change in Your Life.* London: Momentum Press.

Grant, A. M., & Palmer, S. (2002). Coaching Psychology, meeting held at the Annual Conference of Division of Counselling Psychology, British Psychological Society, Torquay, 18 May.

IFERA (International Family Enterprise Research Academy) (2003). Family businesses dominate. *Family Business Review, 16*(4): 235–239.

Lane, D., & Corrie, S. (2009). Does coaching psychology need the concept of formulation? *International Coaching Psychology Review,* 4(2): 195–208.

Mandl, I. (2008). *Overview of Family Business Relevant Issues. Final Report.* Vienna: Austrian Institute for SME Research. Available at: http://ec.europa.eu/enterprise/entrepreneurship/craft/family_business/family_business_en.htm

McCann, G., DeMoss, M., Dascher, P., & Barnett, S. (2003). Educational needs of family businesses: perceptions of university directors. *Family Business Review,* 16(4): 283–291.

Robbins, K. D., Pantuosco, J. L., Parker, F. D., & Fuller, K. B. (2001). Small business. *Economics,* 15: 293–302.

Senior, J. (2007). Life coaching: origins, direction and potential risk—why the contribution of psychologists is needed more than ever. *The Coaching Psychologist,* 3(1): 19–22.

Shams, M. (2006). Approaches in business coaching; exploring context-specific and cultural issues. In: P. Jackson & M. Shams (Eds.), *Developments in Work and Organizational Psychology* (pp. 229–244). The Netherlands: Elsevier.

Shams, M., & Bjornberg, A. (2006). Issues in family business: an international perspective. In: P. Jackson & M. Shams (Eds.), *Developments in Work and Organizational Psychology* (pp. 5–47). The Netherlands: Elsevier.

Stelter, R. (2007). Coaching; a process of personal and social meaning making. *International Coaching Psychology Review,* 292: 191–201.

Stelter, R. (2009). Coaching as a reflective space in a society of growing diversity—towards a narrative, postmodern paradigm. *International Coaching Psychology Review,* 4(2): 209–219.

Stewart, I. J., Palmer, S., Wilkin, H., & Kerrin, M. (2008). Towards a model of coaching transfer: operationalising coaching success and the facilitators and barriers to transfer. *International Coaching Psychology Review,* 3(2): 87–109.

Vadnjal, J. (2005). Developmental orientation of family enterprises in Slovenia. PhD dissertation, Faculty of Economics, University of Ljubljana.

Westhead, P., & Cowling, M. (1998). Family firm research: the need for a methodological rethink. *Entrepreneurship Theory and Practice,* 23(1): 31–56.

Westhead, P., & Howorth, C. (2006). Ownership and management issues associated with family firm performance and company objectives. *Family Business Review,* 19(4): 301–316.

CHAPTER TWO

Recent developments in family business coaching psychology

Manfusa Shams

Introduction

T here has been steady progress in the development of coaching psychology in the UK, but systematic discussion of different types of coaching has not yet been fully undertaken. This chapter aims to present an overview of the recent developments in family business coaching with particular attention to recent innovative coaching practices for family businesses. Examples will be drawn from authors' own personal experiences, and from existing research to suggest future directions for family business coaching.

Research initiatives, institutional movement, and groundwork for coaching—where does family business coaching stand?

There has been an upsurge of initiatives to move coaching psychology to the forefront of practitioners' agendas in order to popularize coaching in the domain of psychology. For example, the special coaching psychology group within the British Psychological Society was set up in 2005 with the aim of developing a distinct area of psychology with an immense practical value, of benefit to both individuals and organizations. Following this project, several other initiatives were developed, such as the "Association of Coaching Psychology" or the "Coaching Psychology Network", together with the development of coaching psychology courses in various universities and private training institutions. Further work to publicize coaching psychology is being carried out through conferences, workshops, forums, and media exposure. These academic and commercial activities are providing the groundwork for the development of coaching psychology in the UK. The movement is in its early stage: family business coaching is yet to take its place in its own right as a distinct coaching practice, encompassing family dynamics and coaching models, with an eagerness to include family psychotherapy and counselling models in practice. However, the challenges between business coaching and family business coaching from a psychological viewpoint need to be addressed so that a complimentary approach, rather than a competitive one, can be considered for the benefit of coaching practices, for businesses in general, and for family businesses specifically. What is promising is the growing interest in establishing family business coaching as a very useful practical tool to benefit both families and businesses. This interest will have a far-reaching goal to the development of coaching practices for the family by the family members.

Innovative family business coaching and global practices

It is apparent that family business coaching is enriched with diverse innovative approaches to meet the needs of local and international family businesses. For example, in addition to appropriate use of psychometric tests, family business coaches use phrases such as "family constitution", "family psychodynamics", and "family counselling". Also, more dynamic and innovative concepts are being constantly taken from related disciplines, such as genogram and ecomap from social work, and family systems from psychodynamics (Shams & Lane, 2008).

The definitive practice for coaching psychology is blended with other sub-disciplines, such as counselling, clinical, health, sports, and occupational psychology; therefore, more novel and dynamic coaching practices for family businesses can be expected. To promote the initiative for developing innovative coaching practices, collaborative efforts and institutional support must be available.

In the absence of a systematic global coaching practice, we have to rely on individual cases to appreciate the need for culturally appropriate family business coaching practices, as well as to trace any issues specific to a culture. I would like to present a case study where business functions are regulated by a cultural-specific framework. The case involves an Asian family business, identified by "X" here. The "X" is run by three generations, where a strong cultural monopoly in the execution of business functions is prevalent. Thus, cultural-patterning business coaching is favoured rather than a general business/executive coaching approach, especially to facilitate and enhance employee performance, with employees mainly from Asian backgrounds. The leading owner of the "X" asserts the importance of the continuity of family tradition and cultural practices in all business functions, and the need for any training and supervision to be carried out within the indigenous coaching framework. For example, the family business "X" gives importance to succession planning at an early stage, with preference for a male leader, equity in share holdings and management, thereby seeking an indigenous approach in running a family business, and for which personal ability and achievement is less prioritized than cultural and family traditions. In this situation, a general executive coaching approach model, for example, coaching benefits pyramid model (Cross & Lynch, 1988), cannot be fully applied to meet the coaching needs of the employees at the "X" organization. If this is so, then a new direction is needed for the coaching model in order to take into account essential issues in culture-specific coaching, and to identify developmental needs using indigenous coaching practices. I would like to encourage our readers to continue discussions in this area.

A good coaching practice for a family business must be based on essential elements of family functions, together with businesses the family owns, governs, and operates. It is encouraging to see interdisciplinary input in the provision of a coaching service for family businesses. For example, there are numerous family business coaching consultancy services around the world, and each has taken a distinct mode of practice, although there are overlapping issues that have not been discussed or researched yet. In the following section, an attempt has been made to present an overview of interdisciplinary contributions to family business coaching.

Interdisciplinary contributions to family business coaching

Unlike any other coaching practices, family business coaching practice is embedded within an interdisciplinary context. An example is the application of a family-centred counselling framework in family business coaching practice. Similarly, economic and legal frameworks, psychometrics, and business studies are often used in family business coaching practice. The question is whether an interdisciplinary input to the development of ethically sound coaching practice can bring about successful outcomes, particularly in ensuring sustainable growth for family businesses. The answer is not straightforward, as there is still not sufficient evidence to indicate the benefits of interdisciplinary input for the development of coaching practice. This issue should be a prime area for further exploration, so as to direct the future of family business coaching. Yet, there is a call to draw clearly defined boundaries for coaching psychology in order to maximize the benefits family businesses may get from coaching sessions that are grounded on psychological principles.

Family business coaching: who is it for?

The burning question is whether family business coaching is for family businesses seeking an intervention for the sustainable growth of business. There are no guidelines or core coaching techniques for family businesses and, therefore, various coaching techniques, such as executive coaching, psychodynamics, and life coaching, are in use in family business coaching practices. The question, however, is to what extent these varied coaching techniques, used to coach family businesses, can serve the purpose of delivering a standardized coaching service for such businesses. The question is further complicated when two strands of family business—"family" and "business" appear to demand independent attention from coaches. Each of these strands must be treated separately in order to get a solid unitary strand of thought for coaching "family business". Thus, family business coaching is for "families" as well as for "businesses operated by families"; in addition, it is up to the coaching profession to value and promote this coaching practice to benefit families, businesses and family business coaching. The best practice in this context is to support family functions to ensure sustainable growth of the family business, which means that family dynamics must be included in coaching a family business. Does this imply that family business coaching is a dual coaching practice, in which family dynamics coaching must be carried out in parallel with business coaching to ensure a smooth transition of family functions to business functions by the family? This does not happen in actual practice. In most cases, the conventional coaching technique is applied to coach a family business, thus leaving a gap in the coaching practice for family businesses. The reason for overlooking the need to coach a family as a social unit may be related to the practitioner's professional background. For example, family business coaches are from diverse professional backgrounds, ranging from sports to chartered accountants; therefore, the need for coaching families independently of business coaching may not get the required attention. This may imply that the responsibility lies with the coaching psychologist to move these strands forward in order to arrive at a coaching technique in which both family and business issues are addressed. The issue may be further complicated by available coaching practices which coaches can apply at their own discretion, based on their judgement of the needs of family businesses.

A coaching model for family business

In the absence of a good coaching model for family businesses, the following working model is presented, in the expectation that it will provoke further initiatives and generate interest in applying this model to family business coaching, as well as to work on developing the model further. The framework can be regarded as the groundwork for future research. The model is generated from the existing topical issues in family business coaching. The aim is to show how the different elements of this model are addressed in each chapter to support the fundamental framework of this model, and to suggest the practicality of this model in coaching practice (Figure 2.1).

Family business coaching encompasses multiple factors and involves complex interactions between family dynamics and business functions. Therefore, effective family business coaching must unpack the complexities in these two parallel areas and pinpoint the issues regulating the sustained growth of a family business. This model has made an attempt to portray the essential steps and interactive processes of family business coaching, derived from discussion by practitioners and coaches in each chapter. It is expected that the features in this framework will develop with increasing practice in family business coaching on the principle offered in the figure, which is that there is a linear relationship between family relations and family business functions, implying that good family functions will lead to effective business functions, and that the success of any coaching practice is based on the effective application of two-tier coaching practices.

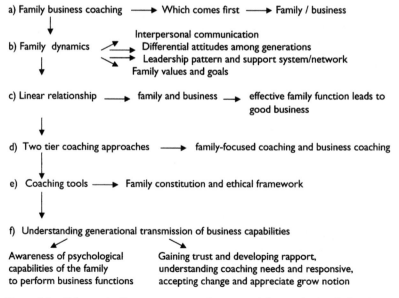

Figure 2.1. Schematic diagram representing essential steps in family business coaching.

The coaching tools in a family business must comprise tangible products, such as family constitution as well as non-tangible yet essential issues emerging from the interaction between family relations and business functions, such as communication style, leadership style, generational transmission of business capabilities, psychological capabilities of family members, gaining trust and developing rapport, family values, and attitudes towards business. All these issues focus on the key question: what comes first—family or business—in a coaching practice for family business?

Each of the major steps above can be grouped together to support the notion of mixed embeddedness (Kloosterman, Leum, & Rath, 2000). The application of this notion to the family business context has been discussed in detail in Shams (2006). Innovative coaching practice for family businesses, adaptation of existing coaching tools for family businesses, and a family-centred coaching approach are well under way in the discussion of coaching psychology. An integrated coaching practice incorporating coaching for families and businesses can address many outstanding issues in relation to family business coaching.

Summary and conclusion

The future of family business coaching from a coaching psychology perspective is still in the developmental stage, although family business coaching in general has been an ongoing practice in the business world. This chapter has argued for a focused approach to address both family functions and business functions in a single coaching session, thereby promoting the concept of a "two-tier" coaching approach, given that the relationship between families and businesses are linear. The chapter has also highlighted the importance of a global family business coaching technique, so that any inconsistencies in coaching practice for family businesses can be ironed out, and the discipline can show its unique position in the coaching arena. There should be increasing dialogues between different coaching practices for family businesses so that a good ethically sound standard can be maintained in family business coaching.

References

Cross, K. F., & Lynch, R. L. (1988). The SMART way to sustain and define success, *National Productive Review*, 8(1): 112–122.

Kloosterman, R., Leum, J., & Rath, J. (2000). Mixed embeddedness: in formal economic activities and immigrant businesses in The Netherlands. *International Journal of Urban and Regional Research*, 23(2): 253–267.

Shams, M. (2006). Approaches in business coaching: exploring context-specific and cultural issues. In: P. Jackson & M. Shams (Eds.), *Developments in Work and Organizational Psychology: Implications for International Business*. The Netherlands: Elsevier.

Shams, M., & Lane, D. (2008). Development of family business coaching skills using action models (Genogram and Ecomap) and family system dynamics framework. Annual Special Group in Coaching Psychology Conference, The British Psychological Society, 17–18 December, Westminster University, London.

CHAPTER THREE

An integrative coaching approach for family businesses

Helen Williams, Stephen Palmer, and Emma Wallace

Introduction

The solution-focused, problem-solving approach provides tangible, goal-focused models for effective coaching within family businesses. Models such as PRACTICE (Palmer, 2002, 2007, 2008) offer a clear, practical structure for discussion and a sequential process for the coach and coachee to follow in order to achieve measurable outcomes. There may be times, however, when the coachee is confronted with psychological blocks or obstacles. In these instances an "intrinsically brief integrated approach" (Palmer, 1997a,b) may be appropriate, whereby Stress Mapping and cognitive–behavioural approaches, such as the ABCDEF model (Ellis, 1994; Ellis, Gordon, Neenan, & Palmer, 1997; Palmer, 2002), are effectively integrated into the solution-focused process in order to increase the likelihood of coaching success (Palmer, 1997a,b).

This chapter provides an overview of the PRACTICE model, Stress Mapping, and ABCDEF model in turn, followed by practical guidelines and an illustrative example to demonstrate how these models may be integrated effectively. A personal account from a coaching client further illustrates the potential power of cognitive behavioural coaching in the family business context.

The PRACTICE model

In the family business context, coachees often choose to focus initially on business issues such as business strategy and challenges, organizational structure and understanding the market, as opposed to more personal developmental issues. Initiating the coaching conversation through the use of a solution-focused framework affords the coaching process crucial credibility before progressing, as and when appropriate, on to more personal goals.

PRACTICE (Palmer, 2007, 2008) is an action-orientated model of coaching that originated as a problem-solving model (Palmer, 2007) and gradually developed into a solution focused model (Palmer, 2008). It is widely used in the contexts of coaching, therapy, and counselling (Neenan & Palmer, 2001; Palmer, 2007). Sequential steps facilitate the coachee in goal identification, consideration of alternative and preferred options, implementation of actions, and review of progress. Discussion is focused, wherever possible, on solution seeking as opposed to problem talk (Palmer, 2008). Table 3.1 provides a description of what happens at each of the seven steps of the PRACTICE model, and questions that may be used to facilitate the solution seeking coaching conversation.

Stress Mapping

Stress Mapping is a visual technique used to help the coach and coachee understand the apparent source of stress in the coachee's situation, sometimes obscured owing to its complexity (Palmer, 1990). Stress Mapping is particularly useful where the coachee will benefit from taking a step back and considering the organizational structure, relationship dynamics, and potential sources and channels of stress. The outcome from the stress mapping process can be increased clarity and an improvement in the level of shared understanding between coach and coachee, a fresh perspective on symptoms and causes of stress, and increased objectivity that can inform subsequent action planning.

Table 3.1.   The PRACTICE Model of Coaching (© Palmer, 2007, 2008, reprinted with permission).

Steps	Questions/statements/actions
1. Problem identification	What's the problem or issue or concern? What would you like to change? Any exceptions when it is not a problem? How will we know if the situation has improved? Any distortions, or can the problem or issue be viewed differently?
2. Realistic, relevant goals developed (e.g., SMART goals)	What do you want to achieve? Let's develop SMART goals.
3. Alternative solutions generated	What are your options? Let's note them down.
4. Consideration of consequences	What could happen? How useful is each possible solution? Let's use a "usefulness" rating scale for each solution where "0" is not useful at all and "10" is extremely useful.
5. Target most feasible solution(s)	What is the most feasible solution(s)?
6. Implementation of Chosen solution(s)	Let's implement the chosen solution by breaking it down into manageable steps. Now go and do it!
7. Evaluation	How successful was it? Use a success rating scale 0 to 10. What can be learnt? Can we finish coaching now or do you want to address or discuss another issue?

Stress mapping is based on systems theory, in that components of a system (e.g., individuals, equipment, ideas, or activities) produce emergent properties that could not necessarily be explained by the individual parts (Palmer, 1990). In a family business setting it is often the case that the system of interest is the soft system, and the components of interest are the interpersonal relationships that make up the formal and informal business structure.

The stress map attempts to quantify the level of stress triggered by components, with the coachee rating the stress on a scale of 0–10 where 0 = no stress and 10 = extreme stress (Palmer, 1990). Arrowheads are used to depict the direction of stress in the relationship, and a + sign is used to depict frequent peaks to a higher than rated amount of stress (Palmer, 1990). Figure 3.1 shows the type of diagram that may be developed through the Stress Mapping process (Palmer, 1988).

In the solution-focused process, Stress Mapping may sit most comfortably in the initial context setting and problem identification steps. However, it may be as you begin to look at realistic goal development that the need to gain further clarity of the situation is identified.

The ABCDEF model

Cognitive–behavioural coaching is based on rational emotive behaviour and cognitive behavioural principles: the assumption that the way people think and feel about events profoundly affects how we choose to behave and perform in response to the event (Ellis, 1994; Neenan & Palmer, 2001; Palmer & Szymanska, 2007). Our reactions to life events are largely determined by our perceptions, meanings,

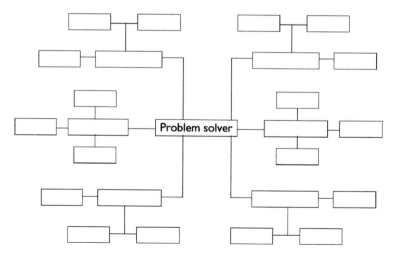

Figure 3.1. Stress Mapping (© Stephen Palmer, 2002).

and evaluations of events rather than by the events themselves (Neenan & Palmer, 1996). Cognitive–behavioural coaching aims to equip coachees with cognitive control over emotional, physiological, and behavioural reactions to stressors (Woods, 1987) and thereby maximize their performance.

Ellis (Ellis, 1994; Ellis, Gordon, Neenan, & Palmer, 1997) developed the five-step ABCDE model of emotional disturbance. This has since been adapted to the six-step ABCDEF model by Palmer (Palmer, 2002) and applied within coaching, counselling, and training. (There are variations to Ellis's model in the published literature.) Table 3.2 describes each of the steps A to F.

While using stress mapping and/or the solution-focused approach, occasionally blocks may occur. For example, it may be that the coachee is holding themselves or the business back due to self-limiting beliefs, is having difficulty asserting business ethics over family values, or is having difficulty letting go and delegating control and responsibility. If performance interfering thoughts (PITs), self-limiting beliefs, thinking distortions and/or emotional

Table 3.2.   ABCDEF model descriptions (© Adapted from Palmer, 1997a,b).

Step	Description
A	Activating event (actual or inferred past, present, or anticipated future). Awareness of problem, difficulty, or issue.
B	Beliefs and images about difficulty. Thinking errors (rigid demands, distorted thinking, self-limiting beliefs).
C	Consequences—emotional, behavioural and physiological disturbances resulting in reduced productivity, performance, and problem-solving.
D	Discussing and disputing beliefs. Questioning whether there is evidence in support of the belief, if the belief is logical and if the belief is of practical use.
E	Effective response. Alternative ways of thinking, feeling, and behaving.
F	Future focus, what has been learnt.

blocks are identified at any point in the coaching conversation, it may be appropriate to side-step into the ABCDEF model at each or any of these times. Rational emotive behaviour and cognitive–behavioural approaches, such as the ABCDEF model (Ellis, 1994; Ellis, Gordon, Neenan, & Palmer, 1997; Palmer, 2002, 2009a,b), can help the coachee to identify their own patterns of thinking, feeling, and behaving, to identify what of this is helpful and what is unhelpful, and to generate alternative ways of thinking, feeling, and behaving. Use of the ABCDEF model equips the coachee with fresh perspectives and the cognitive skills to cope with these more personal challenges, before progressing with the solution-focused process and achievement of their overarching business goals.

Practical guidelines and illustrative example

Problem identification

Open questions and follow up probes are asked to help the coachee specify precisely the problem or issue that they are faced with. The coachee rates the problem or issue with regard to how near resolution they are currently, evaluated on a scale of 0–10, where 0 = nowhere and 10 = resolved. The coach helps the coachee to word the problem in ways that suggest change is possible (Palmer, 2007), building on exceptions to demonstrate the problem or issue is less of a problem overall (Palmer, 2008).

Coach: What would you say is the problem that you are facing currently?

Coachee: It is a business problem; the leadership arrangements are not working.

Coach: How might you word that in a positive way, as a problem that you can do something about?

Coachee: I need to review my leadership arrangements, to consider what the leadership team of the future business looks like.

Coach: How would you rate this problem with regard to how near resolution you are currently, evaluated on a scale of 0–10, where 0 = nowhere and 10 = resolved?

Coachee: I would rate the problem currently at a 3/10; I am some way from resolving this issue.

Stress Mapping

Once the problem or issue and the system in question have been identified (e.g., the interpersonal relationships within the business), a Stress Mapping diagram may be drawn either by the coach or coachee (as preferred by the coachee), using a pre-prepared template or drawing a fresh diagram on A1 paper or a flipchart. The coachee's name is written in the middle of the system, followed by the names of other important components in the outer connected boxes. The coachee rates the relative levels of stress triggered by each component on a scale of 0–10, noting any sources that tend to peak frequently to higher levels by adding a + sign. The coach facilitates discussion of each component during this process, and notes, or asks the coachee to note, any important observations or insights.

Next the coachee rates the levels of stress they perceive that they cause other components in the system. Where further clarity is needed, the coachee is asked to add in the sub-systems of significant components (e.g., "teams" or "departments" or new computer systems represented as whole units, to avoid over-complication). The coachee then steps back and reviews the system and strengths of stress sources within the system, noting down any important observations and reflecting on how they could tackle any stressors or issues that they have now recognized. Finally, the coachee is asked how they found the process, and how the insights will inform their goal setting and action planning. A typical dialogue is below.

Coach: It may be helpful to complete a quick practical exercise at this point. The idea is to map your business as a system and to show the interpersonal relationships within it, with you at the centre of the system. We then quantify the sources and direction of stress causation within the system in relation to your current problem of leadership, so that we can further clarify the issue and identify key actions required. This process is called Stress Mapping. How does this sound?

Coachee: Yes that sounds useful, let's do it.

Coach: Here is an example Stress Mapping template, so you can see what we might aim towards. On the flipchart, draw a box in the centre and write your name in it [Phillip]. Now draw lines to connecting boxes and write in the names of your main relationships [Manager A, B, and C]. Okay, now using a scale of 0–10, where 0 = no stress and 10 = extreme stress, rate the level of stress that each of these relationships causes you [8, 9, and 5 respectively] [see Figure 3.2]. Talk me through these ratings.

Coachee: With Manager A there is a lack of understanding of his team. This causes me difficulties as it means I do not have the insights I need as to the talent in his team. This team happens to have the majority of non-family member employees in it. Manager B is my main problem, however: they hold very strongly to the old ways for our business, that family loyalties should come first, that family members have a right to expect to be promoted into the leadership team. They also represent the majority family member employees and do not assist me in managing expectations here. Manager C is a useful adviser to me and is supportive of the new direction for the business, to be more objective in our leadership selection; however, they are not outspoken about this, as they are sensitive to the family dynamics and different views within the business.

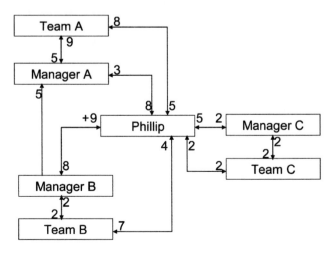

Figure 3.2.   Illustrative example Stress Map.

Coach: You have described how two of the teams have majority family member and non-family member employees in them. It might be useful to add the teams to the Stress Map. Can you now rate the levels of stress coming from the teams to yourself [5, 4, and 2 respectively] and also to the managers [5, 2, and 2]?

Coach: + signs may be used to identify any sources of stress that tend to frequently peak higher than the given rating—would you add any + signs to your Stress Map?

Coachee: Just one, to Manager B in the direction of him to me. He tends to have emotional outbursts on the matter of leader selection during the SM meetings, under the banner of defending the rights of the family.

Coach: Now we can consider the levels of stress that you might be causing others in the system. How would you rate the connections outwards from you to each manager? [3, 8, and 2 respectively] and to each team? [8, 7, and 2]. Would you add any + signs? What do you observe from these ratings?

Coachee: What I had not considered was the impact I am having on others' stress levels. I am a source of stress for the teams because neither family members nor non-family members know where they stand with regard to promotion prospects. Similarly, because I have not made my views and intentions for the direction of the company formal, this causes tension for the managers and places tension on the relationship between the managers. I have no clear vision or strategy with regard to this, or a written policy or clear investment plan for staff development, all of which could help aid the business shift. This all comes down to a lack of communication.

Coach: Why do you think you have not formalized anything?

Coachee: While nothing is in writing, I'm not held accountable to anything, and actually we are not preparing for anyone to take over my leadership role. I do need to commit wholly to what I do actually believe, which is that for the business to survive I must identify a successor. I need to put this in writing as a policy and learn to let go. I am also aware that I have some control issues, in that I do not want to let go! I need help here—I need to learn to trust and to delegate to the SM team and beyond.

Coach: So the mapping process has highlighted a number of additional insights, some of which can inform the practical actions you decide upon, and some of which are more psychological, perhaps more for personal development, such as learning to let go of control, to trust, and to delegate. You have said that you would like help on these points, so if you like we can come back to that in a moment. First, I think it is important that we revisit the problem you have identified and develop some clear goals to work towards.

Realistic, relevant goals developed

The coachee specifies the exact goal using SMART objective setting; Specific, Measurable, Achievable, Realistic, and Timebound (Locke & Latham, 1990; Locke, 1996; Neenan & Dryden, 2002). The goal will ideally be achievable given available resources, specific, realistic, substantial, verifiable, and recognizable as their own (Palmer & Burton, 1996).

Coach: What specific goal might you set yourself now with regard to reviewing the leadership arrangements and future leadership team?

Coachee: To prepare a policy regarding leadership assessment and promotion within the business, to understand our leadership capability in the business now, and to build a succession plan.

Coach: So, how might you make this goal SMART—specific, measurable, achievable, relevant, timed?

Coachee: To write the policy with the SMs involvement by month end; to conduct a review of the leadership capability by year end, to have identified one or two potential successors for each senior leadership role, and to be aware of gaps in our leadership capability.

Alternative solutions generated

The coach asks the coachee to generate and note down as many solutions as possible, no matter how ludicrous these might seem, as from these ideas the coachee may generate a good alternative (Palmer, 1997a,b, 2008). The aim is to encourage creative thinking about alternative options and openness to different possibilities, deferring judgement in order to generate as many varied ideas as possible (Osborn, 1963). Attention is drawn to relevant competence, strengths, and qualities identified in the initial coaching conversations that may be of importance or use to the coachee in generating alternative solutions (Palmer, 2008). If the coachee has difficulty generating solutions, it is reasonable for the coach to offer some suggestions (Palmer, 2007).

> *Coach*:   What are your options here? Be as open as possible and note down all possibilities on the flipchart, no matter how remote.

Coachee writes on flip chart:

1. Hold a senior management team meeting.
2. Complete a desktop review based on my own knowledge of employees.
3. Run an external assessment of all employees.
4. Run the assessment process internally, using the senior management team to evaluate team members.
5. Meet with each employee individually.
6. Get the employees to rate themselves.
7. Assume there is no talent in the business and hire new leaders externally.
8. Follow the family line and allocate family members as successors to all leadership roles.
9. Remain head of the business and maintain leadership control indefinitely.
10. Sell the business.

Consideration of consequences

The coachee is asked to consider the pros and cons of each option in turn, what might happen and how useful each option might be. The coachee then rates each option on a usefulness 0–10 scale, where 0 = least useful and 10 = most useful. Visualization techniques may be used here (Palmer, 1997a,b), for example asking the coachee to engage in time projection imagery (Palmer & Dryden,

1995), visualizing a desired future scenario in which the more desirable option(s) have been undertaken.

Coach: Now let's consider the pros and cons of each of these options in turn, rating each one for usefulness, where 0 = not useful and 10 = very useful.

Coachee: Well, a senior management meeting should be informative, so I would value option 1, although the SMs don't necessarily understand all individuals equally well. I would give a rating of 7; my knowledge is reasonable but more limited than the SMs knowledge, so option 2 gets a rating of 5; we don't have the budget for external assessors although I'm sure this would be the most objective process, I'll rate that 5; running some form of internal process through the SMs is a great idea, 8/10; I don't have the time to meet all individuals, so rating 4; self assessments may be informative, but not in isolation, 4/10; hiring externally would be very treacherous ground, with both family and non-family employees, and a waste of the talent we do have—3/10; we have made the mistake previously of promoting purely on the basis of family ties; I am trying to move the business away from that model, although it isn't easy and not all the SMs are on board. Still, it's the direction I want to take the business in, so my hand won't be forced—I'll rate this as a poor option, 4/10; keeping control indefinitely certainly would be the easiest option! But only if I want to run the business down, which I don't, so I'm afraid that gets a 3/10; likewise, selling the business would be a disappointing outcome and, I hope, unnecessary—2/10.

Target most feasible solution(s)

The coachee is asked to select one or more of the most feasible or practical solutions, with which he or she intends to proceed. Palmer (1997a,b) identifies three key questions to be asked at this stage:

1. Can the problem or issue now be resolved or managed?
2. Do you need more information before taking a decision?
3. Which option/solution(s) should be pursued?

If the answers to questions 1 and 2 are affirmative, then it is reasonable to progress to action planning, revisiting the SMART goal setting, and helping the coachee to break down their chosen solution(s) into manageable, practical steps (Palmer, 1997a,b). If the answer is negative, then time may be taken to explore the issues further, revisiting step 2: realistic goals developed, and/or considering the use of cognitive–behavioural methods where it appears the coachee may be holding themselves back or limiting themselves through cognitive or emotional distortions (Palmer, 1997a,b).

Coach: OK, so considering these evaluations and ratings, which are the most feasible and practical solutions that you would wish to proceed with?

Coachee: I will go with options 1 and 4, holding an SM meeting and asking them to facilitate an internal review—but incorporate option 6 within that, and have the process include self-evaluations.

Coach: How committed do you feel towards taking these steps?

Coachee: Very—I can schedule the SM meeting for two weeks time, get a communication out to employees within one month, and have the leadership capability review complete by year end, as I specified in my goal. I will also schedule a half-day SM meeting for the succession planning itself. I am concerned though, that I will revert to type and try to keep full control of the process. This is when the SMs disengage, at the point that I do not empower them. I find it so difficult to just sit back and watch when they are not running things the way I would want to.

Coach: This is something that you mentioned earlier in our session, that you wanted to learn to let go of control, to trust, and to delegate. If you agree, we can take time to look at this personal goal now.

ABCDEF Model

The coach first clarifies the coachee's development goal and goal/expectations for the coaching session. The Activating event or Awareness of a problem is then identified and noted before typically moving on to consider the current Consequences (feelings, physical reactions, and actions/inactions). The activating event is revisited before moving on to *B* and identifying any unhelpful *B*eliefs or images the coachee holds with regards to the goal. The coach then helps the coachee to *D*iscuss and *D*ispute these beliefs, identifying what is causing the most difficulty and challenging these unhelpful beliefs: what evidence is there to support or refute it? Have there been any occasions on which that has not been the case? How logical is the thought? Whether true or not, how helpful is it to hold the belief so strongly and to live by it? What more helpful thought might be held in its place?

The coachee is asked to generate alternative ways of thinking, developing an *E*ffective response, for example thinking more positively, more flexibly, or taking a different perspective. With emotions, the coachee may monitor how they are feeling, identify and own their emotions, and take an active choice whether to act on those emotions or to let them go. Finally for *F*uture focus, the coachee is asked to hold these new beliefs and imagine themselves in the future, and to then reflect on what they have learned from the process that will mean they are less likely to become stressed by a similar event in the future. Table 3.3 shows the coachee's responses to the ABCDEF model.

Implementation of Chosen solution(s)

The coachee may require time here to go away and implement the specified action plan and may ask for the coach's involvement in rehearsal and feedback processes. The coachee may choose to keep a journal or log of actions taken, outcomes, feedback, and personal reflections (thoughts, feelings).

Coach: It is advisable to keep a log of how you find implementation of these actions, for our review meeting that we can schedule now.

Evaluation

At the evaluation stage the coach and the coachee review the implementation experience. The coachee shares their experiences, feedback, and self-reflections, rating the success of each option implemented on a scale of 0–10, where 0 = not successful and 10 = highly successful. The coachee is encouraged to consider what has

Table 3.3. Illustrative example ABCDEF model (Template © Stephen Palmer, Centre for Coaching, 2008)

Activating event or Awareness of problem	Beliefs	Consequences	Discussing and Disputing beliefs	Effective response	Future focus
Product re-branding, marketing initiative.	Not being done the way I want. Not being informed enough.	*Emotions* Nervousness about letting go of control. Anxious. Frustrated. Angry.	There is more than one way to achieve success, there might even be a better way.	*Emotions* Acknowledge anxiety and anger, defer judgement—there might not be anything to get angry about.	Being aware of how I'm feeling can help me to manage my behaviours.
SM led project.	Don't know what's happening. Losing control.	*Physical reactions* Tense. Sweat. Sleep disruption.	I want to give up control.	*Physical reactions* Re-join gym, exercise as a channel for energy. Usually sleep better after exercise.	Two of my goals are in conflict—to keep control but to have the business survive me.
	It's going to be a failure, the business will fold.	*Behaviours* Micro-manage SMs. Asking lots of questions. Make demands, controlling. Criticize. Change the plan, show who is boss.	If the re-branding is less successful than it could be, it won't be the end of the world.		I need to value my SMs and employees as they are my chance for the business to sustain growth, for me to leave my legacy.
	This must be done perfectly for the business to survive.		The business is strong with a number of products.	*Behaviours* Be clear on expectations and whether I need informing or involving. Listen to ideas. Be respectful. Be open to alternatives.	
	I can't stand sitting back and waiting for things to go wrong. It's inevitable they will go wrong.		I value and respect my SMs and employees; they are learning to be business leaders of the future.		I imagine me sitting calmly in my office, like a wise tribal leader, letting his people learn the way for themselves.

been learnt, and what other actions may now be taken to achieve further success on each option, or alternative options they may now wish to follow. If the coachee rates their success as low on the 1–10 scale, then the coach can explain that the attempt to undertake the possible solution provides useful data that they can now examine together, to understand what got in the way of progress. If the implementation experience was successful, then the coachee may be asked whether there is further coaching required, or whether the coaching may now be brought to a close.

Coach:	In our previous meeting, you identified the goal of understanding the leadership capability in the business and building a succession plan, and specified actions of holding SM meetings around an internal talent review process. How has this progressed?
Coachee:	We have made reasonable progress. The initial SM meeting took place and the SMs have since had 1:1 meetings with their team members. The next step is to have the follow-up SM meeting for succession planning, and then to address the second goal of motivating and engaging the employees.
Coach:	How might you rate where you are currently with the problem of understanding leadership capability, where 0 = nowhere and 10 = resolved?
Coachee:	7/10. We need to have the follow-up meeting. I have also worked on my personal goal of trusting the leaders of the future, which I find I have to remind myself of. This is work in progress, but I know what I want and how to achieve it.
Coach:	Would you like to spend any time today discussing this goal further, or any other goals, or otherwise do you feel we can end the coaching here?
Coachee:	I am happy with the discussions we have had to date and now need to action these. We can end the coaching here.

Personal account

The following case study, written by the coachee, explores her views on how cognitive–behaviourally based business coaching helped her to address her psychological blocks to expanding her business.

I believe that cognitive behavioural coaching helped me in a number of ways. I wanted to expand my business, yet found it difficult to know how. One of the issues I faced was that, as a "one man band", there was only so much I could achieve myself: after all, there are only so many hours in a day. I was however, having to turn work down as I was simply unable to do it all myself. I realized that I was never going to expand my business unless I got other people to help me. My aim, therefore, was to ask a number of carefully selected colleagues, also self-employed, to help me on an associate basis. I also wanted them to appear on my website. The idea was that I could allocate some of my client work to them, hence expanding my capability, while still maintaining control and ownership over delivery. The challenge I faced was actually asking colleagues to become my associates. My main "thinking errors" were that they would not think I was good enough, or at least not take me seriously enough, and would not want to appear on my website. When considering the ABC model of the cognitive behavioural approach, very simply:

1. The activating event was me asking other professionals to join my business as associates and appear on my website.
2. My belief was that they would not take me seriously enough, not think I was good enough.
3. The consequence was that I felt insecure about my abilities and credibility and didn't ask them.

Cognitive behavioural coaching helped me to identify my thinking errors and enabled me to re-frame my thoughts. My coach helped me to understand that my beliefs were having a negative impact on me expanding my business. He identified my thinking error—referring to it as a common thinking trap known as "Phoney-ism": that is, the fear that others may find out we are not the person we are portraying. By helping me to consider what was "in it" for my colleagues in becoming my associates, he helped me to see that I was offering them an opportunity to get involved in the work I do. Reframing my thoughts to ones that more accurately reflected reality, for example, "I have a good range of clients", "I get involved in interesting work", "my clients use me again and again", "my clients want more from me than I can give" enabled me to feel more confident about asking them. I did ask them, and all five professionals in my field said that they would be delighted to become an associate and appear on my website. By correcting my thinking errors through cognitive–behavioural coaching, I overcame my psychological blocks and achieved my goal: I expanded my business, using associates to help me.

Conclusion

Solution focused frameworks such as the PRACTICE model provide a credible and effective start point for coaching conversations within the family business setting. Stress Mapping and the ABCDEF model may be usefully combined with PRACTICE to facilitate a more in-depth and personally focused discussion addressing cognitive, emotional, and/or behavioural blocks if and when required by the coachee. Progress achieved on personal understanding and development through the Stress Mapping and ABCDEF model acts as an enabler for achievement of the overarching business goals.

References

Ellis, A. (1994). *Reason and Emotion in Psychotherapy* (revised and updated). New York: Birch Lane Press.

Ellis, A., Gordon, J., Neenan, M., & Palmer, S. (1997). *Stress Counselling: A Rational Emotive Behaviour Approach*. London: Cassell.

Locke, E. A. (1996). Motivation through conscious goal setting. *Applied and Preventative Psychology, 5*: 117–124.

Locke, E. A., & Latham, G. P. (1990). *A Theory of Goal Setting and Task Performance*. Englewood Cliffs, NJ: Prentice Hall.

Neenan, M., & Dryden, W. (2002). *Life Coaching: A Cognitive Behavioural Approach*. Hove: Routledge.

Neenan, M., & Palmer, S. (1996). Stress counselling: a cognitive-behavioural perspective. *Stress News, 8*(4): 5–8.

Neenan, M., & Palmer, S. (2001). Cognitive behavioural coaching. *Stress News, 13*(3): 15–18.

Osborn, A. (1963). *Applied Imagination: Principles and Procedures of Creative Problem Solving* (3rd edn). New York: Charles Scribner's Sons.

Palmer, S. (1988). *Personal Stress Management Programme Manual*. London: Centre for Stress Management.

Palmer, S. (1990). Stress Mapping: a visual technique to aid counselling or training. *Employee Counselling Today*, 2(2): 9–12.

Palmer, S. (1997a). Problem-focused stress counseling and stress management: an intrinsically brief integrative approach, Part 1. *Stress News*, 9(2): 7–12.

Palmer, S. (1997b). Problem-focused stress counseling and stress management training: an intrinsically brief integrative approach, Part 2. *Stress News*, 9(3): 6–10.

Palmer, S. (2002). Cognitive and organizational models of stress that are suitable for use within workplace stress management/prevention coaching, training and counselling settings. *The Rational Emotive Behaviour Therapist*, 10(1): 15–21.

Palmer, S. (2007). PRACTICE: a model suitable for coaching, counselling, psychotherapy and stress management. *The Coaching Psychologist*, 3(2): 71–77.

Palmer, S. (2008). The PRACTICE model of coaching: towards a solution focused approach. *Coaching Psychology International*, 1(1): 4–8.

Palmer, S. (2009a). Rational coaching: a cognitive behavioural approach. *The Coaching Psychologist*, 5(1): 12–18.

Palmer, S. (2009b). Inference chaining: a rational coaching technique. *Coaching Psychology International*, 2(1): 11–12.

Palmer, S., & Burton, T. (1996). *Dealing with People Problems at Work*. Berkshire: McGraw-Hill Publishing.

Palmer, S., & Dryden, W. (1995). *Counselling for Stress Problems*. London: Sage.

Palmer, S., & Szymanska, K. (2007). Cognitive behavioural coaching: an integrative approach. In: S. Palmer & A. Whybrow (Eds.), *Handbook of Coaching Psychology: A Guide for Practitioners* (pp. 86–117). London: Routledge.

Woods, P. J. (1987). Do you really want to maintain that a flat tire can upset your stomach? Using the findings of the psychophysiology of stress to bolster the arguments that are not directly disturbed by events. *Journal of Rational-Emotive Therapy*, 5(3): 149–161.

CHAPTER FOUR

Intercultural coaching approach for Asian family businesses

Ho Law

Introduction

This chapter aims to show how coaching psychology can be applied across cultures in assisting Asian family business owners to develop their business further in terms of succession and ethical governance. In particular, Law's (2007) narrative coaching approach, within the Universal Integrative Framework (UIF), is singled out to illustrate its applicability within the business and cultural context. We shall first present the reasons for cross-cultural coaching being important for Asian family businesses. Some definitions of key terms on intercultural coaching are provided. This is followed by a description of models of family business evolution and UIF narrative coaching respectively. A case study is provided to show how UIF narrative coaching was applied to help an Asian business owner to further develop his business. Major developmental gaps are highlighted and six ethical principles are provided for consideration to be used for business owners and coaches. Finally, we conclude with some suggestions for future research and developments.

Why cross-cultural coaching is important
for Asian family businesses

Owing to advances in transportation, especially in aviation technology, air traffic has increased many times over. Equally, there has been an increase in the movement of people across the globe and businesses today tend to operate internationally. This trend applies not only to large global corporations, such as HSBC or McDonald's, but also to small and medium size enterprises (SME).

It follows that cross-cultural coaching has been recognized as an important vehicle to enable change in organizations and personal development of business executives internationally (Law, Ireland, & Hussain, 2007; Rosinski, 2003). Applying coaching psychology across cultures is regarded as an important aspect of coaching competence (Law & Yeung, 2009). However, most of the cross-cultural coaching work done so far has been about preparing Western business executives to adopt a cultural-sensitive approach to the local people (for example, see Burch & Houkamau, 2008). There are very few exceptions dealing with coaching for the Black and Asian Minority Ethnic (BAME) entrepreneurs on how to develop their businesses in mainstream Western culture. One example of such exceptional practice was described by Law, Laulusa, and Cheng (2009), in one of their case studies (Case Study 1), where a Chinese entrepreneur was coached by a French coach about developing his business in France.

There is a clear gap for cross-cultural coaching for BAME business owners. This is a very important (and yet neglected) area for the following reasons. First, we are living in a multi-cultural society. Many Western/European societies in the world have a significant percentage of BAME population; the UK is a good example of such a multi-cultural society. By the term "significant", we mean that it is above 5% of the national population.

Second, owing to historical and structural inequality in terms of economic power, BAME business owners face additional barriers to those faced by SME owners. They would, therefore, benefit more from cross-cultural coaching and yet, as observed earlier, high quality, cross-cultural coaching is noticeably absent. Furthermore, research evidence from Shams (2006) asserts the importance of culturally appropriate coaching for Asian family businesses.

Thus, developing a framework of cross-cultural coaching and examples of good practice is not only important for the coaching profession, but also urgently needed for society, and for BAME owners especially, in the current economic climate. The term "high quality" coaching here implies those coaching practices that are evidence-based and grounded in well-established psychological principles. To clarify these principles, some definitions of cross-cultural coaching psychology are described below.

Definitions

In cross-cultural coaching we assume that the coachees embody different cultures due to the fact that they have travelled from another country at a certain juncture of their life journey. Some researchers refer to "intercultural coaching" for coachees who have different cultural backgrounds or with "dual/multi-cultural heritage", which may be subtly different from "cross-cultural coaching" (Law, 2009). The cross-culture in the former category is due to the dislocation of places, while the latter is due to family heritage only.

In this chapter, the terms "intercultural" and "cross-cultural" coaching are used interchangeably. This decision is based on the fact that many Asian family businesses (of the type addressed by this chapter) consist of both categories in their company membership (cross-cultural and multi-cultural heritage).

Both intercultural and cross-cultural coaching is defined as the interaction between the coach and coachee to enhance the coachee's performance and well being in both their personal life and working environment. This chapter advocates a coaching model grounded in psychological principles that are applicable across cultures for intercultural coaching.

The above definition corresponds to those proposed by Philippe Rosinski (2003) and the British Psychological Society's Special Group in Coaching Psychology (Palmer & Whybrow, 2006, adopted from Grant & Palmer, 2002). Cross-cultural coaching psychology is essentially different from other general coaching models in its emphasis on cultural sensitivity and applicability. Based on this emphasis, a coaching model called Universal Integrative

Framework (UIF) is proposed later, but first the specific issues that BAME business owners face will be discussed in the next section.

Applying a model of family business evolution to an Asian business

Table 4.1 shows a model of family business evolution (Gersick, Davis, Hampton, & Lansberg, 1997). It shows how a family business can develop over time through successive generations. According to this model, family businesses develop through a natural expansion to maturity and eventually become a large corporation.

This model can be further expanded to account for two types of family businesses in terms of their development or evolution. Type 1 family businesses are those that maintain direct control of the company (for example, Dow-Jones and Fisher family/The Gap). Coaching business owners through this transition should focus on the company policies to check for any errors of omission or commission that might have impact on their control structure.

Type 2 family businesses control businesses indirectly through share holding. These businesses may or may not have developed through natural progression, but at a certain point of the evolution, they have sold its core business and are just holding on to the majority of shares to stay in control (Table 4.1).

In this chapter, we are focusing on Asian family business owners. This is because from our observation, many Asian business owners (ABOs) are in family business. In addition to this, Asian family values and practices present them with a unique challenge in running the business. For instance, the business shares are usually divided among the family members and relatives of the business owners. Unlike a typical family, a high proportion of Asian business owners do succeed in continuing the same business over the generations (a common example is Chinese and Indian restaurants in the UK). A minority of these businesses may grow so large that they have a number of family branches with shared ownership control and investments. This is because their business values accumulate over the generations. These family businesses that succeed over generations are referred to as "dynasties". For a detailed

Table 4.1.   A model of family business evolution (modified from Gersick, Davis, Hampton, & Lansberg, 1997).

Business	Type	Business form	Mode of control	Strategy	Governance structure
Generation G1: Entrepreneur	0	Entrepreneurship	Founding owner	Personal vision	Ad hoc, implicit
G2: Family partnership	I	Maturing business	Sibling team	Renew business	Informal board, implicit policies
G3: Business dynasty	I	Holding company	Family branches	Sustain profitability; generate new wealth	Board with outsiders, formal policies
G4: Hidden dynasty	II	Diverse portfolio of companies	Shares	Family direction	Voting rights

discussion on major issues in Asian family business from an international perspective, please see Shams and Bjornberg (2006)

Issues facing family business coaching practice

The family values of the ABOs mean that they may fare better in comparison with the mainstream family businesses in terms of succession. However, business succession would still be a major issue that would affect the Asian businesses as their younger generation may take on different values from the mainstream culture and choose to pursue their career aspirations in different directions. More importantly, owing to the different skills, knowledge, and capacity that the ABOs have, the challenges of succession are very different from the mainstream. A good coaching practice must consider these challenges as outlined below:

Succession

As a business develops and matures, the new generations of ABOs may have different personal needs from the founder. For instance, they may wish to break free from the established family business and have a different career or start a new business of their own. Thus, succession is a persistent issue that ABOs face. While in the UK, the changing culture within ABOs over generations begins to show some impact upon their succession; there have been more ABOs facing succession problems in Kenya. Janjuha-Jivraj and Woods (2002) explored the lessons learnt from a number of Asian family businesses in Kenya and found that mothers of the heirs were crucial buffers between the generations. Succession may cause splits between the family members in the business. The experience could be devastating. Thus, long-term planning is an important topic within the business coaching context for ABOs. The strategies to separate management from business are very useful. For ABOs, the challenges in succession include bridging the cultural and generation gaps in terms of understanding the differences in attitude between the generations.

Business governance

ABOs tend to operate in an informal structure. The operation is based on implicit understanding, or by word of mouth rather than explicit terms and condition. Thus, ABOs tend to lack business governance. This situation has prevented many ABOs from getting business funding or loans that might be needed for their business expansion. It also often causes family conflicts when business problems arise.

Generation gap

It is likely that a family business reflects the founder's personal values, aspirations, identity, and attitudes. This idiosyncratic practice is usually passed on to the next generation. However, as the second or third generations grow up, they may have their own aspirations and different values. Over time, the new family members who run the business may not share the same foundation as the first generation. Thus, a generation gap exists, and this may cause further conflicts both within the family and in the business functions. Conflict resolution and an appropriate identity development in relation to family business can overcome these challenges.

Fragmentation

As a result of different values described above, ABOs also run the risk of fragmentation over time. Thus, coaching ABOs on how to integrate different voices of the members within the business is another important aspect. Coaching ABOs is more than financial and business advice.

Application of Universal Integrative Framework (UIF) to coaching an Asian family business

From our coaching experience, we have found that the Universal Integrative Framework (UIF) developed by Law, Ireland, and Hussain (2007) is a generic framework that can be applicable across cultures. This is because the framework was developed from a coaching programme that aimed to address diversity leadership (*ibid.*, 2007). Its definition specifically addresses the cultural sensitivity.

The UIF for coaching developed by Law and colleagues is underpinned by psychological learning theory in a process that is developmental, brings about change, and is culturally mindful. It enables flexibility and fluidity in its practice, extends beyond cultural boundaries, and, therefore, it is useful for coaching ABOs or in any other context where culture is a significant factor that influences the coachee's values.

The UIF consists of four dimensions:

1. Self: represents one's personal competence in terms of managing oneself (self-awareness and self-regulation are two key elements).
2. Social: measures the coach's social competence in terms of managing relationships (key elements: empathy/awareness of others and social skills).
3. Cultural: demonstrate one's cultural sensitivity and competence in terms of managing organizational change (key elements: enlightenment/awareness of other cultures and championing organizational cultures).
4. Professional: defines one's own professionalism by embracing all of the above three dimensions (including continuous professional development and providing feedback).

One of the advantages of adopting the UIF model is that it allows coaches to link a specific coaching technique flexibly to the four dimensions. For instance, from our experience in coaching ABOs, we have found that linking the narrative coaching approach to the cultural and self dimensions of the UIF is particularly useful. Owing to their cultural preferences, many ABOs like to tell a story about their journey of setting up their businesses, their successes as well as lessons learnt from the challenges that they have come across. This makes sense, as theoretically, narrative coaching is grounded in cultural anthropology, which was not only concerned with non-clinical population, but also with specific sensitivity of cultural issues. The narrative coaching approach consists of the following steps (adopted from Law, 2007):

1. Description
2. Relation
3. Evaluation
4. Justification
5. Conclusion.

Step one: Description (characterization of initiative). At this stage, the coach invites the ABOs to tell a story that is based on their experience, for instance, specific events during the course of their business development. In doing so, the coach guides the ABOs to identify the barriers to achieving their business objectives, and talk about their problem-solving skill to overcome them.

Step two: Relation (initiative in relationship). From these stories, the coach helps the ABOs to establish a chain of associations between the events described. The coach maps the impact of the identified barriers on to the significant domains of the coachee's life-story—for example, migration from one place to another, business start-up, fund raising, marketing, succession, and these domains reflect on their values and self-identity.

Step three: Evaluation. Towards the end of the coaching session, the coach guides the ABOs to reflect on the lessons learnt from those relationships and evaluate the outcome.

Step four: Justification. Evaluation and justification steps are interwoven in practice. During the evaluation, the coach challenges the ABOs to justify their decision. In doing so, the ABOs rediscover certain concepts about their life and identity.

Step five: Conclusion (recommendation). To complete the coaching session, the coach guides the ABO to formulate a plan of action. This action plan consists of a set of SMART objectives that further enable the coachee to predict the outcome of specific actions. The action plan can also be integrated within the business plan that the ABOs may have. Depending on the timing of the coaching sessions and the business cycle of the coachee, it may become part of the ABO's annual business review.

A case study

A case study is presented to demonstrate how narrative coaching works for ABOs. This case study is based on coaching a successful ABO who has been in business (and is still going strong) for over thirty years. Although the case study reported is a real-life story, the name of the coachee is made fictitious for confidential reasons. Permission has also been sought for publishing this story.

Mr Singh is an ABO who owns a photography studio in Birmingham. He was educated in India and immigrated to England in the 1970s. He was invited to describe his experience of setting up his business and share his knowledge with the local business community. Mr Singh described his struggle during the business start-up phase, which was supposed to be a simple route. He remembered many challenges that he faced, for instance, arranging finance. Getting a loan from a bank was extremely difficult as he did not have any security to offer, which was essential when asking for a loan at that time. The issue of not being able to obtain a loan was an obstacle.

"Without capital, nothing could be started," Mr Singh recalled with emotion.

Narrative coach: "How did this affect your business?" (attempting to establish a chain of associations and consequences in the plot).

"There are a number of implications as a result of lacking the capital," Mr Singh replied. "For instance, finding a suitable and affordable premises to establish the business, and marketing ..."

Narrative coach: "How did you overcome these problems?" (directing the coachee to identify skills and solutions).

"In order to minimize the start-up costs, I kept the advertisement of my business to the minimum, relying mostly on word of mouth. Later on, I took my business plan and shared it with one of my colleagues, and managed to secure a loan from him," replied Mr Singh.

Narrative coach: "What other challenges did you face?"

"In addition to the normal challenges that any businesses would face, I also experienced some form of racial discrimination. For instance, some potential customers refused to use my services . . ." Mr Singh recounted with a hint of sadness in his eyes.

Narrative coach: "Why?" (seeking justification).

"I think this was because they had a negative perception about the quality of the work that was associated with my ethnicity," Mr Singh explained.

Narrative coach: "And yet, judging from the business success that you enjoy today, you must have the skills that enabled you to overcome this cultural barrier . . ." (attempting to evoke the inner strengths that the coachee might have, without reinforcing the emotion associated with those barriers).

"I did not let it be a barrier. I worked even harder and paid attention to the quality of my work. When people saw the photos that I developed in my shop window, the quality of the work spoke for itself . . ." Mr Singh spoke proudly.

Narrative coach: Were there any other barriers linked to your ethnicity?"

"Yes, the language was another barrier, as English is not my first language. I spoke English with a strong accent, which further reinforced the negative perception that the potential customers might already have about my ability," Mr Singh continued.

While listening to Mr Singh's story about the difficulties that he experienced, the coach not only acknowledged those experiences (showing empathy) but also expressed admiration of how he overcame those difficulties (identifying and drawing on the signature strengths that the coachee had). Despite all the challenges, Mr Singh did not give up and demonstrated great depth of resilience and perseverance. He continued to hold on to his vision and succeeded.

Many other strengths were identified from this person's journey. The coachee was aware that as he was new to the UK, he did not have a track record or references for himself or his business. To overcome this barrier, he did a lot of personal development and learnt about marketing. He took the initiative to advertise his business himself. This included posting leaflets through people's doors and putting them on people's cars, placing posters in pubs, and speaking with the local community and residents in the neighbouring streets, where he would tell them face to face about his business.

From identifying Mr Singh's signature strengths, the coach guided Mr Singh to utilize these strengths and identified the business gap in the photography market. The gap existed because the community comprised many Asians, people who had emigrated from countries such as India, Pakistan, Kashmir, Bangladesh, and so forth. These people came from a working-class background where the opportunity of education was very limited. Therefore, their English was not very good and all tended to speak in their mother tongue. Mr Singh attracted these customers, as he could speak their native language and provide a service for them without their being made aware of the limits of their own communication/language abilities. Thus, he transformed his initial weaknesses (language barrier) into his positive strength (language skills), which became his unique selling point.

Furthermore, as a result of guiding Mr Singh to focus on his customer needs, he recognized that the needs of the Asian customers were different from those of the white customers and he took full advantage of this. For example, many Asians like to have their family portraits taken to send back to their families in their home country. But, because they came from a working-class background, in the pictures they wanted to reflect that they had attained some wealth by being in England. As a result, Mr Singh used to have suits in his store, so that customers could wear them to look smart and give the impression of success.

Narrative coach: "Wow . . . this is an excellent idea. How does this resonate with any particular values or beliefs you hold in high regard? If so, what are they?" (Attempting to guide the coachee to reflect, and evaluate the options that link to his value and self-identity.)

"I think my drive to make the business a success actually stems from a sense of deeper responsibility that I have as the eldest in my family.

Not only do I have a wife and three children to support in the UK, I have my mother, father, three sisters and a brother to support in India. From this I can say that my greatest strengths are my *love for my family, fulfilling my duty as the eldest, sacrificing my time and, in effect, my life by working ten hours a day so that my family can have a better standard of living.* This provides me with strength and self belief that I have the ability and drive to succeed, that it can be done no matter what obstacles are put in my path." Mr Singh spoke reflectively. His voice contained a sense of excitement and positive emotion.

The coachee's self belief led to him to see new possibilities opening up for him. Although there are franchises such as Max Spielman, and photo processing being done at Boots and various other chain stores, his business has an advantage because it is well established and it has maintained a positive reputation from the very beginning. Most of this reputation stems from the fact that he offers a diversity of services including: digital processing, portraits, creating frames for photographs, posters for businesses, restoration work on old photographs, printing images from mobile phones, transferring video tapes on to DVD, selling camera equipment and albums, creating wedding cards, etc. Mr Singh began to recognize the shift in the market and to this day continues to introduce new technology and services to cater for the customer's changing wants and needs. For example, he saw that the market was shifting from still photography to video filming. As a result, he bought the necessary equipment and began to offer video filming services for events such as weddings, birthdays, christenings, and so on. This would not only expand his customer base, but also give him a very good reputation in the area where he was operating. By the same token, the introduction of new technology such as digital software and hardware and using programmes to restore photographs required him to undertake training at various colleges (another action point included in his business plan). By implementing his action plan as part of the business strategy, Mr Singh's business went from strength to strength.

The above case shows that the narrative coach was able to apply the UIF framework to the coaching situation by mapping the coachee's cultural values with coaching techniques and thereby selecting a culturally sensitive coaching approach—in this case, a narrative approach. Furthermore, the coach applied the approach flexibly to the coachee's context, whether it was their business domain or family life.

Ethical consideration

Many business owners believe that ethics simply involves "learning what is right or wrong, and then doing the right thing" (McNamara, 2008). ABOs are no exception. Moreover, as they tend to rely heavily on the family network in their businesses, they tend to neglect the wider implication of ethical principles to their business. However, it is vital for ABOs to develop an understanding of the ethical principles in order to provide a corporate governance for achieving long-term sustainability.

According to UIF, a culturally sensitive way of introducing ethical principles to the ABOs' business practice via coaching is to link them to their cultural values. Law (2010) developed six ethical principles (called the six Rs) which were adopted as the Code of Ethics and Practice for the Society for Coaching Psychology).

These are:

1. Right
2. Respect
3. Recognition
4. Relationship
5. Representation
6. Responsibility

The principles of rights and respect are interwoven in coaching practice; they are usually expressed together as one. The ethical principles listed above can be integrated into the coaching practice as follows.

- Rights and respect: respect the rights of human beings. ABOs should seek *permission* from the customers about using their information for various purposes such as marketing. They should maintain *confidentiality* of their customers, and be *open* to respond to their requests for information. These arrangements should form part of the company policy in line with legislation such as the Data Protection Act. The customer should be made aware of the policy. ABOs should be well placed to be culturally sensitive to their individual customers' cultural differences in terms of their age, gender, disability, race, religion/belief, and sexual orientation, etc.

- Recognition: business owners need to recognize the standards and limits of their business services. They should not claim business values beyond what they can deliver.
- Relationship: establish good relationships and trust with their customers as well as business and family members. Business owners need to establish a rapport with their customers and maintain a good relationship throughout their business development. Employee relationships may be more complicated in ABOs coaching when many family members are involved. ABOs need to be mindful about these multiple relationships, clarify the company roles, and resolve any business and/or family conflicts that might arise in the boardroom.
- Representation: business owners need to represent their business accurately and honestly. They should not act in a manner that might bring their company into disrepute.
- Responsibility: business owners should take responsibility for themselves, the stakeholders, and the company. They need to have business insurance to protect themselves and their business liability. They should encourage family members and employees to take their own responsibility for achieving the business objectives. The business owners are responsible for monitoring and evaluating the overall success of the business and keeping appropriate records for accounting purposes. The business owners should also take responsibility for any unethical behaviour by employees. In addition, the business owners should continue to learn and develop themselves and their businesses.

The coaching practice for Asian family business can be guided by the following questions:

- How ethical is a family business as a whole?
- What are the core values underpinning an Asian family business?

In summary, a coach must understand different cultural practices in family business, and provide coaching appropriate to a particular cultural framework, irrespective of family set-up. The coaching practice will be enhanced and effective if universal ethical principles in coaching can be incorporated along with specific issues concerning Asian family business.

Conclusion

This chapter has shown the importance of using cross-cultural coaching frameworks to assist Asian business owners to achieve their business potential. We have identified the Universal Integrative Framework, using the narrative approach as a useful method in terms of generating meaning and linking it to the six ethical principles. A primary task for coaching ABOs is to help their businesses to continue creating wealth. This is not simply about giving advice on investment or how to diversify the business assets for the family shareholders, but more about how to challenge the decision-making process, take a consensus, and manage emotions in those decisions made by the family. The following areas have been identified as requiring further research and development:

- coaching for wealth creation;
- coaching for sustainability;
- coaching for unity/integration;
- coaching for accountability/governance (ethical coaching, principles of responsibility: see Law, 2010).

The discussion in this chapter has justified the need for an intercultural and universal framework for coaching family business with distinctive cultural orientations, such as Asian family businesses. The need for developing deep insights into the contextual and cross-cultural factors in coaching practice has also been highlighted.

Acknowledgements

The author is grateful to his trainee psychologist, Khushbir Singh, who provided the material for the case study.

References

Burch, G. St. J., & Houkamau, T. (2008). Cultural sensitivity in coaching: with reference to New Zealand Maori. *Coaching Psychology International*, 1(1): 9–11.

Gersick, K. E., Davis, J. A., Hampton, M. M., & Lansberg, I. (1997). *Generation to Generation: Life Cycles of the Family Business*. Boston, MA: Harvard Business School Press.

Grant, A., & Palmer, S. (2002). Coaching Psychology Workshop, Torquay, 18 May. *The Annual Conference of the Division of Counselling Psychology*, British Psychological Society.

Janjuha-Jivraj, S., & Woods, A. (2002). Successional issues within Asian family firms—learning from the Kenyan experience. *International Small Business Journal*, 20(1): 77–94.

Law, H. C. (2007). Narrative coaching and psychology of learning from multicultural perspectives. In: S. Palmer & A. Whybrow (Eds.), *Handbook of Coaching Psychology*) (pp. 174–192). Hove: Routledge.

Law, H. C. (2009). Applying psychology of learning to coaching across cultures. Paper presented at the 4th Annual International Conference on Psychology, 27–30 May 2010, Athens, Greece. Athens Institute for Education and Research.

Law, H. C. (2010). Coaching relationships and ethical practice. In: S. Palmer & A. McDowall (Eds.), *The Coaching Relationship* (pp. 182–202). Hove: Routledge.

Law, H. C., & Yeung, L. (2009). Cross-cultural coaching psychology—a fruitful dialogue. *Coaching Psychology International, Society for Coaching Psychology*, 2(1): 17–19.

Law, H. C., Ireland, S., & Hussain, Z. (2007). *Psychology of Coaching, Mentoring & Learning*. Chichester: Wiley.

Law, H. C., Laulusa, L., & Cheng, G. (2009). When Far East meets West: seeking cultural synthesis through coaching. In: M. Moral & G. Abbott (Eds.), *The Routledge Companion to International Business Coaching* (pp. 241–255). Hove: Routledge.

McNamara, C. (2008). *Complete Guide to Ethics Management: An Ethics Toolkit for Managers*. Available at: www.managementhelp.org/ethics/ethxgde.htm

Palmer, S., & Whybrow, A. (2006). The coaching psychology movement and its development within the British Psychological Society. *International Coaching Psychology Review*, 1(1): 56–70.

Rosinski, P. (2003). *Coaching Across Cultures*. London: Nicholas Brealey.

Shams, M. (2006). Approaches in business coaching; exploring context-specific and cultural issues. In: P. Jackson & M. Shams (Eds.), *Developments in Work and Organizational Psychology* (pp. 229–244). The Netherlands: Elsevier.

Shams, M., & Bjornberg, A. (2006). Issues in family business: an international perspective. In: P. Jackson & M. Shams (Eds.), *Developments in Work and Organizational Psychology* (pp. 5–47). The Netherlands: Elsevier.

CHAPTER FIVE

Dealing with relationship issues in a family business from a coaching context

Elspeth May

Introduction

F amilies are something all of us know something about, even if we know nothing of business. There are moral and social obligations that bind us closely to our family. There is something tribal about being part of a family: it affects our sense of identity. We think of a tribe as being a group of people who have a feeling of association with each other; perhaps an association of ideas as in a political party, or of feelings when we see football supporters dismissing the claims of rival "tribes". Feeling part of a tribe brings us together and, with its association of shared history and genetic material, the family "tribe" is arguably the one to which we are always bound physically and emotionally.

In a family business, it is not just about the business. It is also about the family.

All employees and directors are part of the same business tribe, but only some are part of the family tribe. Whether you are a member of only one of those tribes or both makes a lot of difference. As a coach working with clients in family businesses, you are likely to find that much of your work is related to how the client deals with those differing "tribal" relationships.

The relationship context

The ways in which family businesses are different to other types of business are set out in Chapter Three. The varying aspirations of different family members have an impact on their relationships with each other and it will greatly help a coach working in such businesses to get a good grasp of these relationship dynamics early on in their work. In particular, you need to be clear about the following points.

- The differing expectations of business owners—those who may want income, those who may want capital gain.
- The differing timescales that family members may have in mind for their involvement in the business.
- Possible sibling rivalry.
- Family members working in the business while other family members are not doing so. This can create different reward needs.
- Family directors and non-family directors. This is the area that I shall focus on in this chapter by contrasting the situation of two family members working together (father and daughter) with a case study showing what can happen to a non-family member trying to exert influence in a family business.
- The lack of formal processes and clearly articulated objectives when it comes to performance appraisal and succession planning can make the position of a non-family director, in particular, rather vulnerable.

In many respects, these factors are merely part of the context in which a coach has to work. However, one particular factor can create a difficulty for a coach if it is not dealt with appropriately at the outset, and that is the matter of being clear about who is the client.

Who is your client?

Most business coaches are remunerated by the organization for which their client works, rather than by the individual themselves.

As a consequence, the organization is part of the contract which the coach makes with their client/coachee. That contract is not only a tangible written agreement with legal consequences, but also a psychological contract that the client, coach, and organization enter into. I refer below to the person representing the organization as the sponsor.

For each party to the contract—client, coach and sponsor—there may be different expectations of the contract and I have set out some of the possibilities below. It may be, of course, that some of these expectations are unrealistic.

Client

- The coaching will be confidential. No feedback will be given to the sponsor or anyone else about the content of the coaching discussions.
- The coach is competent and has experience of working with people like me.
- I want us to have some clear goals for what we are trying to work on together.
- The coach is on my side. They will have my interests at heart.
- If anything that comes up in our discussions is beyond my coach's competence, they will refer me to someone else who can deal with that.
- I will feel safe working with this coach.

Sponsor

- I want to know what the coaching will deliver.
- The coaching must deliver measurable results.
- I expect the coach to be competent.
- The client is happy to work with this coach and feels there is good rapport between them.
- I want to have feedback from the coach about how the coaching is going. I am interested in their views on the client's capabilities.
- The client must not become dependent on the coach. This cannot go on forever.

Coach

- There is rapport between the client and me.
- I feel capable of working with this client.
- I am clear about the boundaries for our work and, in particular, the need to keep our discussions absolutely confidential.
- The client will "engage" with our work, not cancel sessions, and will work on our agreed agenda between sessions.
- My invoice for the coaching will be paid promptly.

A couple of examples may help bring these points to life. When I was asked to coach a director who was being considered as a potential managing director in a business, the existing MD frequently sought to brief me on what he perceived were the characteristics required of his successor. He felt that my client did not want the job, although capable of doing it. I had to make it clear to him, at the outset, that, though I might seek his feedback in order to understand what progress the MD thought he was making, I could never reveal anything my client told me, including whether or not he would throw his hat in the ring and compete for the job against other internal candidates. In effect, I had to contract with both my client and his MD as to how we would work together.

A second example occurred when I was coaching a director who was the son of the CEO and was then asked by the father if I would also work with his daughter, who held a senior position in the business. The father felt that with my knowledge of the family and the business, I would make a good coach for his daughter. I declined his offer, referring the work instead to a colleague. While it can sometimes work to have one coach work with several directors in a business, I believe the boundaries are sorely tested if those directors are also siblings; there is too much potential for conflicts of interest. It seemed to me simpler to not put myself in that place.

While these issues are present in all contracting situations, I think there is often a greater degree of interest in the coaching from a sponsor in family business situations. In my experience, this is especially so when the client is the son or daughter of the business founder and the spectre of succession is ever present. This was certainly the case in Case Study 1. (In both case studies I have changed the exact details of the client and their business in order to preserve their anonymity.)

Case study 1

I was asked to coach the daughter of the founder of a packaging business ("Helen"). Her father had created a successful company during the previous twenty years. He had prospered through good economic times and bad and saw himself as an entrepreneur, well respected in his local business community, with an ego strongly supported by the outward manifestations of his success.

Helen had greatly benefited from that wealth and had never had to look for work in earnest, as her father had given her a job in the company. In doing so, he believed that she should start at the bottom and work her way up. He had insisted that his daughter spent the first few years working in the factory, so that she would understand all aspects of the packaging business. She showed herself to be good with people. Her colleagues enjoyed her sense of humour and appreciated her willingness to roll up her sleeves and get things done. But they did not take her seriously as a leader in the business. Her father had too strong a dominance on the decision-making for that to happen.

Recognizing that he would eventually have to let go of the reins and allow Helen to take over the business, the father decided to promote her to commercial director. It was around that time that I was asked to coach her. Her father was pretty sceptical about the value of coaching. Partly because of this, and also because I wanted to see first hand the man who had so much influence on my client, I requested a meeting with the father. This was with Helen's full agreement.

It was apparent at the meeting that the father felt his daughter was not sufficiently interested in the business for him to feel confident that she could one day take over, and yet he genuinely seemed to want Helen to do that. At the same time, it was clear that he would never step down; his sense of identity was much too strongly entwined with that of being head of the business. I came to see that while the coaching agenda I had agreed with Helen was about her being seen as a credible successor for her father, I would stand a better chance of making progress with that agenda if her father were supportive of it. In that sense, he had to be part of the contracting process, albeit via an informal contract rather than one made explicitly.

Having introduced this case study in order to illustrate some points about contracting, I am now going to take it a stage further and use it to illustrate some of the issues which can arise when coaching family members.

Issues in coaching family members

Why should coaching someone in a family business be any different from coaching anyone else? After all, as any coach knows, you are working with the client's agenda, so surely it is only a matter of understanding what that agenda is and then getting on with it?

In one sense that is true; however, I hope that by focusing on some of the issues which frequently emerge when coaching family members, you will be able to identify the right agenda for your client and recognize other issues—perhaps the real agenda—as they emerge.

Developing your own style if you are the son/daughter of the founder

It can be especially hard for the sons and daughters of business founders to escape the sense of obligation that may be placed upon them—explicitly or not—that they will become involved in the family business. In Case Study 1, there was never any question in the father's mind that his daughter would follow him into the business and one day run it. When I started the coaching, Helen talked a lot about how she had resented being made to start at the bottom and work her way up in the business. She had done relevant training and gained business-related qualifications, but these seemed to count for little with her father.

Much of the early sessions was spent exploring what she wanted from life. I did this by gradually asking ever more probing questions (over a number of sessions) to enable Helen to face up to her deeper feelings. This also proved to be quite a painful process for her and brought out a large measure of her self doubt. Helen was shrewd enough to realize she had been given what many would consider to be an easy start in life, but she also felt that she was not "qualified" to do anything other than work in the family business.

I encouraged her to do more networking outside the business. She already had some useful contacts and by taking the lead in contacting them, rather than waiting for their call, she gained in confidence. When they started inviting her to events, she went along, and in one session we talked through how she would like to conduct herself at a forthcoming business dinner. This enabled her to attend that event with greater confidence and, when we reviewed how she had got on, her increased energy and confidence was immediately apparent. She had started to prove to herself that she could be a businesswoman in her own right, not one forever in the shadow of her father. By enabling her to feel safe to confront those inner thoughts, she gained a stronger sense of her own identity.

Gaining the respect of non-family peers

In case study 1, I used the Myers–Briggs Type Indicator to help Helen understand more about her personality and how this manifests itself in her desire to create better systems in the business. As he built the company, her father had been almost entirely focused on bringing in new business, so it had grown without many of the formal systems which larger organizations take for granted.

As the newly appointed commercial director, Helen had to chair the commercial team meetings. She found this exceptionally hard at first, not least because many of the team were older than her and had been more senior to her until relatively recently. Mindful of her Myers–Briggs type, we worked on how to get a better structure for those meetings. After only a couple of meetings of working with a properly structured agenda, clear reporting back accountability, and good time management in the meeting, she started to gain the respect of her team. They could see that she operated in a different way to her father and that that could be effective.

This need to prove that she had gained her position on merit, not just because she was a family member, remained a theme throughout our coaching. Many of the longer-serving staff liked to tease her, and, every so often, she would rise to the bait and show her anger. Helen also had a tendency to withdraw to her office and avoid people who had upset her. I decided to introduce her to transactional analysis in the hope that this would help her understand how patterns of behaviour had been established early in life and were continuing to be played out. She quickly grasped the parent–adult–child model and we talked through how there was a repeating pattern of "critical parent" and "adapted child" in her dealings with her father. When he was critical of her performance, she tended to give in to his proposed courses of action and it reinforced her sense of "not good enough". In one of our sessions, she told me of an instance when she had stood up to her father and given him feedback about a business proposal. As she described what happened, it was clear that the role of critical parent and adapted child had reversed, since her father sulked for several days after that incident and would not speak to her.

Using this model did not resolve her difficulties overnight, but it did help to raise her awareness of when others' behaviour (especially her father's) was triggering unhelpful responses. She gradually learnt to be more measured in her responses and, when difficulties arose, to deal with them in an assertive manner, rather than hide away.

Dealing with succession

For any founder of a family business, there comes a time when you have to think about letting go: whether or not you are going to do it and, if so, when. For the son/daughter hoping to take over, how will they signal their readiness to do that while recognizing the loss of power, status, and sense of being needed which the outgoing founder may feel? This is one of the trickiest issues which family businesses face.

It is very hard for an acorn to grow under a great oak tree. It does not get enough light and nutrients. Recognizing this, many children of business founders decide to pursue their careers elsewhere initially. Their experience enables them to make better judgements about whether they want to join the business. The client in case study 1 had never worked elsewhere and was acutely conscious of that. We had many discussions about whether she should leave and work elsewhere. I used a force field analysis in one of our sessions to work through this dilemma: what were the forces in favour of her staying and what were those in favour of leaving? As readers may know, such a tool does not just look at pros and cons, but at the relative strengths of those forces. I have found that mapping out the forces at play on either side of a dilemma often helps clients see which of them really matters and it enables them to consider the relative significance of each factor to them. Using this enabled Helen to see that there were more reasons to stay in the business than to go, and she became enthusiastic about working out how to stay on her own terms.

It is perhaps worth just pausing a moment to reflect on the particular uses of psychometric and other tools in the context of family business succession and governance. I believe that tools are only useful if they help clients better understand themselves or the situation they face. Understanding one's preferences using the Myers–Briggs Type Indicator (and particularly the Step 2 version of this, which provides a much richer picture of the person than does Step 1) helps clients to think through whether they want to make career changes. For example, if someone is considering whether to try to become the CEO of their business, knowing their preferred ways of working may help them reflect on how they will cope with the challenges of the more senior role.

Similarly, by using transactional analysis, I find clients can acknowledge and then let go certain behaviours which may be limiting their ability to take on more challenging roles—what are sometimes referred to as self-limiting beliefs. This is particularly the case in a family business context where the parent–child relationship may be present both literally and figuratively. This sometimes manifests itself as overly controlling parents who struggle to let their offspring take up the reins of the business, even where they can be considered by any objective criteria as quite capable of doing so.

As I mentioned above, I had a meeting with Helen's father at the start of our work together, but after a few months, when she had decided she did want to stay in the business, I suggested we had a three-way meeting with her father. I proposed that I should act as facilitator, not coach, and that the conversation would be about succession. It would provide an opportunity for Helen and her father to share their hopes for the future and to say what support they would like from each other. It took a while to set up this meeting, as there was wariness on all sides (including my own) as to whether or not it would work. We agreed clear boundaries around the discussion and a short agenda outlining the topics we would cover.

When it came to the meeting, the father inevitably took the lead. I was surprised at how openly he talked about his difficulties in stepping back. He made some suggestions about ways he could do this in certain areas in the business, but also stated that in other areas he would retain control. This was not quite what Helen wanted, but at least her father was being clear. For her part, I was disappointed at how little she engaged in the discussion. It seemed as if her father was willing to step back, but she was not willing to step forward.

I gave her feedback about this at our next session and challenged her on just how badly she wanted to take more of a lead in the business. She asserted that she did, yet kept blaming her father for the lack of progress. We explored this by confronting her choices and the things over which she did or did not have control. As a result, she embarked upon a series of conversations with her father during which they began to talk in more detail about the future structure of the business and their roles in it. While there were no quick fixes, it was a major step forward that Helen and her father were talking about the business together.

Case study 1 illustrates some of the dynamics of a father–child relationship in a family business, together with some of the coaching techniques which can be used to help address these. Relationship dynamics are very different, however, when they involve two directors, one of whom is family and the other is not. This is increasingly common in larger family businesses where there has been recognition in the past that new talent needs to be brought in to the business to supplement the talent that is home grown. Often, the non-family director's desire for autonomy and the chance to "get on with it" and deliver what the business needs of them will be stifled by the family directors' desire to hang on to control and do what they think is best for the *family* more than for the business. Case Study 2 deals with just such tension.

Issues when coaching non-family members in a family business

Non-family directors will be all too aware that they are not "family" when it comes to certain business decisions, most notably concerning succession planning. Many family business owners have a preference for preserving the bloodline in the senior management, rather than let "outsiders" take this on, no matter how capable they are on paper. Case study 2 explores these issues and highlights the importance of clarity about line manager expectations and the principles which are laid down in the family constitution (if there is one.)

Case study 2

I was asked to coach the Finance Director (FD) of a family business. Over many years working in the business, the FD (whom I shall call William) had made his way up the promotional ladder via the finance function. The business was chaired by the son of the founder, and he took a very hands-on approach to his involvement in the company. The business had faced some ups and downs over the years in its trading performance and had reached a point where it badly needed to expand its product range as the markets for its primary products were diminishing. William had some ideas about how they could do this, and, as part of his desire to have a greater say in how the business was run, he was endeavouring to engage the chairman in a dialogue about future strategy. He was even entertaining ideas about taking over the running of the business when the chairman decided to step down.

Our coaching agenda was initially about how William could assert his authority as FD of the business when he had a chairman who was so actively involved. The situation was compounded by a lack of clarity as to the chairman's future plans: would he step back from the business one day and retire? The chairman was never willing to be drawn on this subject. He seemed to be hoping that one of the next generation would show an interest in the business and thereby provide his route to succession. But all his children and those of his brother (who was not involved in the business) were pursuing careers elsewhere.

Initially, our work centred on getting a good understanding—for me and William—of his impact as a leader. I spent a couple of days meeting his team and gathering feedback about him. A clear pattern emerged. He was highly regarded by his team as an effective leader who also encouraged their development. But they were unclear about the strategic direction and often felt uninvolved with shaping future strategy.

William felt frustrated that his contribution to the business was not fully recognized. The chairman seemed continually to nit-pick William's work, ignoring his successes and focusing just on the things that had yet to be achieved. William greatly valued his involvement in the company, but was beginning to question whether he had a long term future there. William and I explored his options.

- Accept things as they are (the "put up or shut up" option).
- Change the environment, which might include systems and processes in the business, or changes to his team.
- Change yourself—either what you do or how you think about the situation.
- Leave.

William quickly ruled out the first and last options. He liked the business and, apart from the uncertainties around future succession, he was happy to stay. So we worked on the second and third options.

Changing the environment meant William learning to delegate more to his team so that he could think about future strategy and find ways to engage the chairman in dialogue about that. Through challenging him about the functions he needed to have in his team, he created a new structure and set about getting the chairman's agreement. We also looked at what he was good at. I adopted a solutions focused approach to get him to think about the times he had delegated effectively and we reviewed what had worked so that he could start replicating that. I made a point in each session of asking William about what had gone well since I last saw him and invited him to list which of his strengths he had been deploying. From his feedback, I know this helped him maintain his self-belief during a pretty stressful time.

This case study illustrates some of the issues related to coaching non-family members, as outlined below.

- *Blood is thicker than water.* Perhaps it is to be expected that many people who have nurtured a business, especially when they have done so from its "birth", will have a strong desire to pass on the business to a member of their family. That can leave the non-family member feeling like an outsider. As Leach and Bogod say in their *Guide to the Family Business*,

> . . . there are many instances of talented (non-family) managers (in family businesses) who have resigned because they have run out of opportunities, or because the politics and emotional cross-currents . . . have become too much of an interference in their work. [1999, p. 52]

From a coaching perspective, this may well mean that the client will want to work through their future career options and decide whether they wish to maintain their career in a family business setting. Exercises like "ideal job" can work well here, whereby you guide the client through a reflective exercise in thinking about what their ideal job would look like. By encouraging them to engage all their senses in the exercise—"What do you see yourself doing in five years time? Who are you with? What can you hear? And feel? And even smell? And taste?"—a rich vision of the future emerges. This can act as a powerful catalyst in helping the client fulfil their wishes.

- *Understanding how the family constitution works.* Not all family businesses will have a constitution, but some will. It is generally advisable, especially where there is more than one generation involved in the business and there are non-family members in key positions. The constitution sets out how the business will be run and deals with matters on which voting may be required and how sales of shares will be managed.
It is sensible to ask for a copy of the constitution and read it early on in your relationship with the client and, indeed, this would be true if you were coaching a family member as well as someone who is not part of the family. But I have included it here as it is likely to have particular bearing on any succession planning that may well be part of the coaching agenda if you are working with someone at board level.
- *Unwritten codes of behaviour.* If there is no formal constitution document, there may nevertheless be unwritten norms and "codes" of behaviour by which the family conducts its

business. A coach may only find out what these are by talking to executives in the business, family and non-family members alike, who have been involved in it for some time. It may be that a coach may suggest to their client that it would provide greater clarity all round if a written constitution were drawn up, but one must be careful here to stay on the right side of the boundary between being a coach and being a consultant with expert knowledge. A coach is not an adviser, but may be able, through skilful questioning, to encourage the client to raise the issue with the rest of the family. The advice of a lawyer well versed in family business matters is essential to getting the right end product.

- *Managing expectations of the client's line manager.* While this can be an issue in any coaching assignment, it may have a particular significance in a family business setting. In case study 2, the chairman wanted to meet me early on (part of the vetting process I suspect, but also he wanted to give me some feedback about William). This helped me better understand the dynamics of William's relationship with him and I would recommend that any coach working in a family business should try to meet as many of the key family players as possible.

  As in any good contracting, I managed the chairman's expectations about the feedback he would get from me about the coaching. None, as far as the content was concerned, but I was willing, if asked, to provide feedback about the number of sessions we had had. During the three years or so I worked with William, I had three meetings with the chairman, always with William's knowledge and agreement. The third of these was a three-way meeting in which we shaped out the next phase of the coaching agenda by seeking the chairman's feedback on the progress William had made to date.

- *Dealing with succession.* In case study 2, the lack of clarity about the chairman's future intentions was a major obstacle to addressing future succession for the running of the business. Had there been stronger non-executives on the board, they might have applied a bit more pressure on the chairman to make his intentions clear, in the interests of the long-term health of the business. In the absence of this, William and I explored his attitude to taking over the business—did he really want the top job? Although as FD he was heavily involved in all commercial aspects of the business, the chairman effectively acted in an executive capacity, restricting William's autonomy. One of the possible structures I discussed with the chairman was for him to move to a non-executive chairman role and let William become the Chief Executive. I suppose it must have been a reflection of his lack of trust in William's ability to take hold of all the reins that he never let them go.

I found myself very curious about why William stayed in the business. I challenged him about his expressed frustration and not having more control, yet he seemed content to accept the situation. Eventually, he admitted that to leave and go out in to the marketplace to find another job was a pretty scary prospect. He was well paid, after all, and he enjoyed the business challenges of his job. His family was settled in the area and he did not want to risk disrupting them by the possibility of a move elsewhere.

I asked a series of questions about outside activities he might pursue. What was his external network like? What types of activities did he enjoy away from the office? What would he like to do in that context? From this emerged a desire on William's part to find a suitable non-executive role. He explored the possibility of a school governorship role and coincidentally (or was it serendipitous?) was head-hunted for a non-executive directorship in a business in another sector. It dawned on William that he did have value outside the business and that others were interested in his views. This, too, helped to boost his self-confidence.

When it comes to self-belief, I find positive psychology very useful, especially the work of Martin Seligman (Seligman, 2002). In particular, I find his model of how our beliefs affect our actions helps clients understand that they can change their beliefs in order to achieve a more positive outcome and, to do that, you need to look at the evidence which is supporting the belief. With William, his sense of "not good enough" was fuelled by some of the chairman's comments. When William and I looked at the evidence of what he had achieved in the company—outstanding business results, loyal customer base, good employee feedback, external awards—it helped him gain a better balanced perspective on his capabilities.

Keeping the momentum going

As coaches, we only get to work with clients for a limited period. So, how do you help the client maintain the momentum for their development after the coaching has ended? Some of the ways clients have addressed this include the following.

- Finding a buddy or critical friend who will offer feedback on perceived changes in behaviour.
- Getting a mentor with whom the client can meet periodically. This may be someone more senior in the business, or someone from outside it.
- Keeping a journal to record their development journey.
- Using affirmations to reinforce new behaviours. For example, repeating "I am competent and confident" before important meetings that might have triggered doubts in the past.
- Keeping a scrapbook/cuttings file of their key achievements.
- Taking stock once a year of what they have achieved and what they would still like to achieve in their career. Is the family business where they want to be?
- Meeting with their coach less frequently, to review progress and deal with any new issues.

Mostly, it is about making time for reflection, something that inevitably happens in coaching but when the coach is not present, can the client keep that habit on their own? They will stand a good chance of doing this if they practise some of the actions listed above and, especially, if they have someone—a critical friend, mentor or coach—who can periodically hold them accountable for their progress.

Relationships in family businesses: summary

Reflecting on these case studies and my other experience of working with family businesses, I realize that *all* the coaching conversations I have had in that context have been, at least in part, about relationships within the business. In this chapter, I have set out some of the issues coaches need to think about when working in this territory and to show, through two case studies, how they can be approached. There are other aspects of family business life that I have not covered: for example, the impact of sibling rivalry on CEO succession or on the way in which family relationships outside work have an impact on those in the business. But I believe the principles that I have dealt with here have broader resonance.

A coach can have a vital role to play in a family business. By being an independent confidante, the coach can enable their client to have a different kind of conversation than they may have with their colleagues and relations. When family members and non-family members are each trying to work out whether they can contribute to the business while retaining a sense of their own distinctive identity, and if so how, coaching provides thinking space to explore this. I have found that, often, those who work at a senior level in family businesses get little support for their development. Providing them with the opportunity to articulate their hopes and doubts and manage the internal relationships can be hugely energizing. It also helps clients recognize that they have a choice. Many family businesses are benevolent places to work and can, therefore, be hard to leave. Helping clients separate their feelings about the family from their feelings about the business, their own career, and their own sense of identity is in the interests of the business and their own, whether or not they are part of the family.

There is much scope for coaching to play a bigger role in family businesses. As I said at the start of this chapter, it is the "family" part of these companies which makes them distinctive and it is not easy for the family themselves to step back from their situation and think objectively about the future of the business. This, combined with the desire to leave a legacy for future generations, means that an independent expert, skilled in understanding human behaviour and the distinctive way this manifests in families, can be invaluable. As ever, the coach helps to hold up the mirror to the situation and challenges the client (and the family of which they are a part) to take the right decisions for the future of the business, not just in the interests of the tribe.

Acknowledgements

The insights which I have gained as a coach have come, in large measure, from the clients and colleagues at Praesta, with whom it has been a great joy to work. A huge thanks to all of them—you have taught me far more than you realize. My greatest thanks go to my husband, Brian, who provides endless support, encouragement, and delicious meals to keep me going as I work. He is the centre of my family and my love.

References

Leach, P., & Bogod, T. (1999). *Guide to the Family Business* (3rd edn). London: Kogan Page.
Seligman, M. (2002). *Authentic Happiness*. London: Nicholas Brealey.

CHAPTER SIX

Family first or business first: issues in family business

Hande Yasargil and Lloyd Denton

Introduction

In every family business, there are the people at the centre, people at the margins, and others in between. Working as coaches to the leaders of family businesses throughout Turkey and the Middle East over the past decade, we have enjoyed many remarkable relationships and learned some useful perspectives, tools, and processes. This chapter is about sharing what we have learnt so far, opening it to discussion and debate, and, therefore, learning more from the experience of other families and consultants. Of course, the details of any cases and examples provided here are altered to protect the privacy of our clients.

Seen from the edges: a family and a business

Coaches working with the complexities of a family business may have good reason to ask the question: what comes first in a family business, family or business ?

One of the most valuable lessons for us has been the importance of knowing our place at the periphery. Equipped with professional knowledge of business and coaching, and of family systems, we tend to spend our time looking in from the edges, choosing carefully when and how we might intervene to create a positive impact at the centre. In fact, it seems to us that some of the most serious mistakes to be made with family businesses arise from coaches mistakenly believing they are at the centre. In this highly complex environment, distance and humility go a long way towards success. Pity those who believe they have joined the inner circle, who are sure they understand everything that is going on, or who become inflexible and doctrinaire in the methods they use or the solutions they apply.

What is a family business?

Who are family, and what is family business? Flexibility is required from first principles, since the idea of a family business—and for that matter the idea of a family—is culturally situated and ambiguous. Examples of ambiguity come quickly to mind in "Western" and "modern" contexts. Divorce, single parenthood, and same-sex relationships certainly add complexity in some family business arrangements. But a clever Turkish therapist once observed, "You can't assume a family is functional, just because it is strong." Coaches may be equally likely to encounter ambiguities and complexities among traditional Eastern families and their businesses. Real-life examples from our experience include blood relatives ostracized from a family for dishonourable behaviour, and a child given in undocumented adoption between sisters. In both cases the unquestionable authority of a family elder decided the matter, and a degree of uncertainty remains about what complications might develop when that elder dies.

As with art, people tend to know who the family members are and what a "family business" is, even if the particulars of a definition are a little difficult to nail down. Often, a strong entrepreneur starts a company that functions, succeeds, survives, profits, and grows. Then, for reasons of preference, availability, or cost, they involve one or more family members—spouse(s), children, siblings, even in-laws. Does it matter whether those family members hold shares, draw salary, or have executive titles? From a coaching perspective, we find an inclusive definition most practical: a business in which more than one member of the same family is *a significant presence* is a family business. For example, a father hires his son, who is not a university graduate, into a salaried job. All his peers in the same role have a degree. Whether the son is a shareholder or not, there is an impact on the culture and on the company's reputation for fairness. When the boss's wife comes into the office twice a week to review the receipts and check the bookkeeping, it shapes the power dynamics of a company even if she does not draw a salary.

These situations become management issues with business impacts. As the influence of family dynamics will be experienced in virtually every organizational context, business coaches are well served to develop awareness and expertise in this area even if they do not brand themselves as "family business specialists".

Family frames and lenses

Family is the frame through which we perceive and interpret any subsequent human relationship. Organizations are structures of relationships regulated by purpose. People devote much of their waking lives to one or more organization, beginning with the family, then school, and later the organizations in which they work. As societies become more complex, people are called on to individuate from the family, and play a wider variety of roles in more and more organizations, including roles that can overlap or conflict. Still, even in organizations that have a very different purpose or structure, people tend to be reminded of and influenced by the family: their experience of its communication patterns, roles, functions, dysfunctions, expectations, and frustrations.

We recreate, relive, and rework these family patterns in many new and different situations. For example, it is common to see sibling rivalries carried over into professional competition. People with authority, such as the school principle or a CEO, may resonate with memories of a father, be they warm or cold. Men may perceive something of their mother's attentiveness in their wife's affection, or something of her control in the insistent enquiries of a female co-worker. As a result, they may respond in a way that once led to success in the family environment, but fails in the context of a different organization with a different purpose. Interestingly, they usually do this without being aware they are mirroring their family experience. When acting on influences that are beyond their awareness (i.e., unconscious influences), clients can often benefit from the objective observations and challenges of a coach.

The influence of family patterns on later relationships and the need to gain an appropriate level of independence from the family system are still present, and greatly complicated in a family business. This is true for family members themselves, of course, but family businesses also create a more complex environment for employees, and especially the professional executives who are often called upon to share family feelings of loyalty, responsibility, and ownership while also keeping their place as outsiders. Our role as business coaches is often to foster the development of leaders, facilitate change in the organization, and challenge and support both the professional executives and family members. Almost always the goals are about sustainability and business outcomes.

An integrated coaching model

Our metaphor for an integrated coaching model is a visit to the ophthalmologist's office where there are many frames, lenses, and scopes at hand. In dialogue with the client, we explore different combinations to determine which lenses bring the most clarity. Often, we adjust the view in small increments, zooming in and out, and checking for a comfortable fit. Sometimes a correction is required, other times not.

As coaches we join our clients in looking at their business cases through a variety of frames and lenses. As we partner with them to meet their challenges, to raise awareness, and add value to the business, we have found a mixture of tools and approaches helpful. Our practice has been shaped by personal business experience and by our studies in coaching and family business with Manfred Kets de Vries, Randel Carlock, and others at INSEAD. Studies in brief therapy and pastoral counselling have also contributed. Most of all the collegiality of the Praesta organization—where a regular dialogue with ninety executive coaches working in twenty countries fosters continual learning and exploration among reflective practitioners—has shaped our integrated coaching model.

By integrated coaching model, we mean a coherent approach that lets us apply to any particular business case a whole range of insights from the different disciplines that now make up the knowledge base of the coaching profession. A partial list of perspectives that might inform our work on cases could include competitive strategy models, decision theory, emotional intelligence, cognitive–behavioural theory, adult learning theory, appreciative enquiry, personality theory, group dynamics, leadership studies, change management, institutional governance models, and our own experiences in business leadership. Without compromising the "no harm" principle, we are continually sorting out what works best through experience and reflection, and sharing the results with our peers. While there may always be an element of intuition in the process, we continually work on our ability to integrate various approaches in an explicit and systematic way that can be evaluated, criticized, and, therefore, improved.

Psychodynamic theory is consistently useful in our work with family businesses. It offers the vocabulary for many patterns we observe, such as regression, transference, projective identification, narcissistic defences, sibling rivalries, and more generally the role of the unconscious. While we are clear that our coaching work is not about pathology, diagnosis, or therapy, we do draw on the knowledge base of psychodynamic theory to inform our analysis and our work with clients.

One pattern of behaviour we often encounter is a defence mechanism described in psychoanalytical theory as "regression". People regress when faced with a conflict they find too stressful or difficult to deal with, or when their usual approach to a conflict or problem fails. Regression means that they revisit earlier attempts to resolve such challenges, returning to behaviours previously given up as ineffective or immature (Kets de Vries, 2001) While everyone else in the room may see it clearly, clients themselves are not aware of their shift into regressive behaviour. When confronted or given feedback about the pattern, they may resist discussing it, as they often experience this as embarrassing or disconcerting. Regression is, after all, an *unconscious* defence. One of the alarming things about regression is that it can trigger behaviour that seems not only immature, but also to contradict the client's very identity, as it were. Regression can appear sudden and out of character. Because regression triggers behaviour that is out of character, a coaching model that focuses exclusively on the identification and enhancement of "strengths" can meet with its limitations here. Sparking insight and raising awareness through comparisons with "when you have used this sort of behaviour before" gets to the issue in a psychodynamic frame. A coach can use the cognitive–behavioural toolkit to explore and interrogate what underlying assumptions may surround a particular episode. Is another way of thinking about the triggering factors possible? Personality theory may also shed light on these reactions. The Challenge Report, based on the Hogan Development Survey, is designed to identify leadership derailers across eleven risk dimensions. Clients have found this tool helpful in understanding the regressive behaviours they are likely to fall into when challenged to their limits. When stressed or threatened, do they, as Karen Horney theorized, move towards people in an effort to please, move against people in an effort to intimidate, or move away from people in an effort to escape (Horney, 1950)?

Another way that unconscious associations with family experience come into play is through transference, the unconscious redirection of feelings for one person towards a different person. Being attentive to transference is vital in any coaching situation. A good definition of transference from the psychoanalytical perspective is "the inappropriate repetition in the present of a relationship that was important in a person's childhood". This includes "the redirection of feelings and desires and especially of those unconsciously retained from childhood toward a new object".

According to Kets de Vries (2001), we are all prone to a kind of confusion between current and past relationships:

> . . . what transference says is that no relationship we have is a new relationship; all relationships are coloured by previous ones. . . . As we relive those earlier, primary relationships again and again, stereotypical behaviour patterns emerge. [p. 73]

As coaches, one valuable area of work is helping clients to achieve greater awareness of those "stereotypical patterns" in relationships and to leverage their awareness to create the kind of change they desire for themselves. We sometimes use a "life and career timeline" tool that inspires clients to write/draw the story of their relationship patterns along with other key elements of their personal history. Other coaching exercises focus on the objective discussion of depersonalized "roles" to establish rational expectations, and then compare with the client's real experience. As clients discover more about patterns in their experience of relationships, a coach can help them keep this learning in mind and challenge them to be aware of the choices they are making.

Although transference reactions happen in all kinds of relationships, working relationships sometimes reveal them in starkest relief because of their functional and hierarchical nature. For example, one of our young MBA students recently described how she successfully managed an authoritarian boss who bullied her coworkers:

> "One day I told him I felt like his little daughter. Even though he yelled at me, I knew it was for my own good and I was not going to take it personally. Instead of confronting him with inappropriate behaviour or resisting, I would shut up for a while or just disappear when he got upset, and later act as though nothing happened. After a short time he really started to act like my father, he started to protect me from difficult situations; he started to advise me about the future, and he even apologized for the times he shouted and lost control. With this kind of positioning I survived his very stressful management style, and even benefited. But on the other hand, when it was time for me to leave the company I felt like I was betraying my family by leaving them."

This brief and very common case demonstrates both transference, and projective identification. Our first question to the student was "What motivated you to stay with this boss and find a solution to the problem, when some of your colleagues preferred to find another job?" She was proud of her ability to cope with the situation, but was unaware of the real similarities between her own family patterns and the management style of her boss. She was familiar with the role she adopted at work through her previous experience as the manipulative daughter of a very dominant and controlling father. The reason "projective identification" is involved here is because, in response to her behaviour, the boss did actually begin to "protect" as if he were her father.

The importance of these concepts and others from the psycho-dynamic knowledge base, such as narcissistic needs and sibling rivalry, make themselves apparent in many family business engagements.

In an integrated coaching model, the psychoanalytical tradition, while useful, is only one of the lenses to be applied. When we think about the business organization as a system and begin to intervene at the relationship level, the lens provided by family systems theory can refine the view. Family systems theory gives us concepts such as homeostasis: the tendency of the organism to seek and maintain a condition of balance or sameness within its internal environment, even when faced with external changes. From family systems theory, we may use other useful concepts referenced in the cases below: wholeness, family rules, the feedback process, subsystems, and so on.

Key to systems theory is a refusal to analyse a single individual without reference to the context in which she lives and works. Our model reflects this insight in that we always strive to inform the process of coaching at various points, with data from multiple stakeholders: boss, peers, direct reports, human resources; and often from key business partners, customers, or family members. Today, we see that coaches working in the corporate market will be required to balance value provided to the individual and the organization by using information from throughout the system to increase the impact of coaching.

We understand people better by seeing them as a part of their whole system as one player among others in the relationships and interactions that make up a functioning organism. From this perspective, family businesses tend to be rich and complex; and in working with them coaches will want to raise awareness about the roles and relational patterns in the family system and in the business organization. Other details also inform systems analysis. Factors such as a client's gender, birth order, class, education, and physicality will often play an influential role in their stories, as will the status of their family, tribe, or ethnic group, or the collective memory of their early successes and failures. In the coaching conversation, or when shadowing a client in the work environment, there is an art to deciding what is significant to observe, to mention, or to reflect upon further while *not mentioning*. Catching what is most significant and noting what is significantly absent often requires both business experience and a solid theoretical background.

More lenses and frames

In recent years, a great deal of work has been devoted to the concept of narcissism in management literature. For our purpose a simple observation is enough. A *single driven entrepreneur* is very often at the heart (or in the history) of a family business, and coaches should not ignore the possible influence of narcissistic needs and narcissistic personality characteristics among such people. Indeed, strong entrepreneurs come in many stripes, but clinical studies have shown that a significant number become what they are because of what drives them (Kets de Vries, Carlock, & Florence-Tracey, 2007). They are sometimes striving to remedy past hurts by proving that they are a "force to be reckoned with" in the market, in the business, and in the family.

> Children who have been exposed to inadequate or dysfunctional parenting may later believe that they cannot depend on anyone's love or loyalty. . . . These are people who, despite their claims to self-sufficiency, are troubled in the depth of their being by a sense of deprivation, anger, and emptiness. In order to cope with these feelings, and perhaps as a cover for their insecurity, some people allow their narcissistic needs to turn into obsessions, becoming fixated on issues of power, beauty, status, prestige, and superiority. They can end up with grandiose sense of self-importance, require excessive admiration, have an unrealistic sense of entitlement, can be interpersonally exploitative, and are unable to recognize or identify with the feelings of others. Furthermore, their attempts to manoeuvre others into strengthening their shaky sense of self-esteem makes them appear manipulative and arrogant. In many instances, people with narcissistic disorders are preoccupied with thoughts of getting even with the injuries that they experienced while growing up and they can be extremely envious. [Kets de Vries, Carlock, & Florence-Tracey, 2007, pp. 86–87]

The often-repeated doctrine that proper coaching deals with future successes rather than "past hurts" always seems inadequate to us in the face of certain real challenges presented by leaders who fit this profile. A well-trained coach can become aware of a client's narcissistic needs and adjust the way they position themselves accordingly. It almost goes without saying that someone who is not aware is not likely to adjust. With these individuals, a coach is more effective if she can see a pattern and adapt to avoid the defence, or use the energy of that defence to effect positive changes. For example, a coach may want to be especially careful in scheduling and administration details to avoid any perception of inattentiveness or neglect with clients who demonstrate narcissistic needs. Similarly, in emphasis, a focus on visionary thinking and the planning of future success might support feelings of grandiosity, while directly confronting unrealistic statements could cause a narcissistic client to disengage quite suddenly.

On yet another level, coaches can increase their likelihood of success not only by adjusting to the individual and system dynamics, but also through awareness and flexibility in the face of cultural differences. Each family and each organization has its own unique character, and what functions well in one leadership context can falter elsewhere. From the margins, outsiders can easily miss the impact culture makes if we jump to conclusions or forget our core practices of openness, humility, and listening. Something similar can be said of national or regional cultures, the difference being that our coaches are not always "outsiders" in this regard. But whether they carry the same passport as their clients, or a different one, an awareness of local culture and its impact on business leadership remains critical.

Family first or business first?

The question "family first or business first?" is about organizational culture. In many family enterprises the family relationships take priority, and the business is a secondary concern. In such a paradigm, the very purpose of the business is to support and empower the family. In other cases, the needs of the business predominate while family relationships take a back seat. In this view, ideas about objectivity, fairness, and scientific management often ring-fence business operations, sheltering them from what may be seen as less rational (or unnecessarily complex) family concerns. Of course, the relative value of family or business can also shift in different circumstances, or from generation to generation, or individual to individual. Still, coaches working in a family business system would probably be well served to ask or to assess whether business comes first, or family comes first. This balance can determine almost every key decision in a family enterprise. With a "family first" approach, an enterprise may encounter challenges in communication, as well as talent and career management. For example, open communication and confrontation become more risky in an environment where certain roles simply are not going to change. Lack of communication is one of the most consistent issues we encounter in family businesses, both in terms of inability to communicate and intentional strategies of non-communication. In businesses of this kind, coaches can add value by encouraging and modulating communication, and by calling attention to the need for fairness when it comes to talent and career management.

A company will probably seek to employ competent professional managers, but may find it difficult to motivate and retain them if the most desirable positions are earmarked for next generation family members, or if a confusion of reporting lines and bloodlines complicates the management task. In "family first" style businesses, the problem can become more pronounced when family members and friends (in reality or in perception) take positions they are not best qualified to hold.

On the other hand, in an economy where relationships accomplish as much as actions, the notion of "qualification" takes on a different meaning. In many businesses in this region you find one group whose members' qualifications reside primarily in their relationships, including a trusted relationship with the family business owners. A separate group is qualified as a result of its members' education, competence, and track record in the relevant business. Comparing the treatment of family members, trusted professionals, and competent professionals often leads to conflict and misunderstanding. The perceptions of unfair treatment that stem from prioritizing what is good for the family can create resentment and undermine the contributions of "the professionals".

"What do leaders look like around here?"

The question "What do leaders look like around here?" is about national or regional culture. It is a topic that deserves a chapter in its own right—volumes, in fact. Designated leaders who fail to live up to people's perception of what they should be experience a degree of pushback from the group. Regardless of their choices and intentions, they may find what they do is always already inscribed into the leadership narrative expected by others. Stepping outside the accepted path can be quite a challenge. Leaders who set out accomplish change projects, ranging from implementing "corporate governance" to driving "customer focus" initiatives, often feel the organization pushing back. They may intend to lead differently, but must face the deep-seated expectations of others about "what a leader looks like around here".

As business partners from two different cultures, and as business coaches working with local and expatriate executives in eight countries, we have pondered and researched this issue and have a great deal to say. However, we find that lessons about coaching, leadership, and the cultural distinctiveness of Turkey and the Middle East are best shared in a living dialogue. The one-sided discourse of a book chapter can lead to misunderstandings and raise sensitivities. It is enough to say that many of our engagements rely on rapport and honesty across significant differences in nationality, religion, gender, station, and world view. In these circumstances, positioning and authenticity are everything, despite the irony. The chance of success relies on the coach's confidence to be herself, her awareness and sensitivity to the cultural expectations, and on her ability to raise these issues at the right moment for explicit discussion and contracting. And, as with every other dimension of the coaching relationship, success ultimately depends on the client's openness and willingness to engage.

Who is the client? Where is the coach?

Who is the client? is an enlightening *koan* for therapists and coaches alike. A mother goes to a therapist and complains about her son's laziness. A coaching client has only one presenting issue: her boss does everything wrong. A CEO wants his team coached because they are not aligned. In each case the answer is simple. The client is always the complainer, since a complaint indicates the energy needed to work on a problem (Weakland & Segal, 1982).

We always *consider* the whole system when coaching in family businesses. This is different from actively involving all the players.

Instead of insisting on working with all the family members, we often start work with the complainer alone. Along the way, if we find it helpful or if there is a demand from the others, we may invite or accept other family members as active participants in the coaching process, but always with the agreement of the initiating client.

Where is the coach? We believe the coach's role in family business settings may sometimes need to be more directive or active than with individuals. It is more complicated to work with multiple realities and multiple agendas in family business settings, so the coach may choose to leave his non-directive position from time to time and take a consultant, trainer, or a catalyst role, as long as he clearly returns to the original position. The same shifts in positioning are advocated by many in family therapy. Coaches are not necessarily trained as family therapists, and may find it safest to stay out of the system, while remaining system-aware. But depending on the skill of the coach and on the openness of the client(s), the coach may also use his position in the system as a useful intervention.

Conclusion

As living systems, families have their histories, conflict patterns, roles, boundaries, scripts, and usually a skeleton or two in the closet. Those realities predate our involvement and will live on long after coaching concludes, though we might hope in a slightly altered configuration. Working with families requires special expertise, and is not simply a subset of group coaching or facilitation work. Coaches will almost certainly find basic psychoanalytical categories and some family therapy research useful in family business engagements. Additionally, developing knowledge and respect for the cultural context in which leaders function is critical. This holds both for the organizational culture and the prevailing cultural norms in a given society. One of our mentors is fond of saying that all families face exactly the same problems in amazingly different contexts—business and cultural contexts. What is consistent is that that they have generations, and that they struggle with meeting the needs for both love and work. In family businesses, people have much stronger feelings about each other and about the business than we find in other companies, where relationships can be more easily dissolved. Coaching families without a sound understanding of those dynamics may not only fail to be helpful, it may do significant harm.

As coaching develops, there is a rich variety of discussion about professional ethics, methodology, and technique. Early turf disputes are becoming more sophisticated conversations about how coaching can best draw from the knowledge base of other disciplines, such as psychotherapy, without losing its own integrity and identity. Coaching is neither management consulting nor psychotherapy nor executive education, but good coaches can use resources from each of those disciplines in a thoughtful, reflective practice.

Acknowledgements

The authors wish to acknowledge Manfred Kets de Vries, Randel Carlock, and Roger Lehman of INSEAD, David Lane of Middlesex University Professional Development Foundation, and Peter Hawkins of Henley Management College and our colleagues at Praesta for the many ideas and the powerful encouragement they have offered. Thanks also to Dr M. Shams for her skillful editing and persistence.

References

Horney, K. (1950). *Neurosis and Human Growth*. New York: Norton.
Kets de Vries, M. F. R. (2001). *The Leadership Mystique: A User's Manual for the Human Enterprise*. London: Prentice Hall.
Kets de Vries, M. F. R., Carlock, R., & Florent-Tracey, E. (2007). *The Family Business on the Couch*. Chichester: John Wiley.
Weakland, J., & Segal, L. (1982). *The Tactics of Change: Doing Therapy Briefly*. New York: Jossey-Bass, Social and Behavioral Science Series.

CHAPTER SEVEN

Exploring a coaching approach for expatriate family businesses in an international context

Elisabeth Legrain-Frémaux

Introduction

Couples and families living in an expatriate situation have a unique opportunity to explore the potential to start a family business. Creating change in individuals or groups normally requires the creation of a sense of urgency to shift people from compliancy and/or fear. Expatriates referred to in this chapter are executives in a leadership position on international work postings, working across countries and cultures. These personnel are posted overseas, most of the time on a voluntary basis, motivated by job advancement potential, opportunity to travel, and a higher income. Most expatriates only stay in the foreign country for a certain period of time, and plan to return to their home country eventually, although there will be some who choose to stay on and never return to their country of citizenship.

Their world has been turned upside down and inside out, and they have to start building a new family life in a new country, often with a different language and a very different culture.

This can be an amazing opportunity to dig in unexploited resources and to transform them into something new. For an expatriate spouse, or their whole family, it can be to try that business initiative that has always been "too risky" or "too challenging". The journey that the expatriate family takes towards setting up a new family business outside of their home country can be made easier by moving forward with special care and also by getting appropriate support, such as coaching.

The chapter will look at the unique opportunities presented by the expatriate situation, which are listed below.

1. Relatively high disposable family income compared to working in their home country.
2. Spouse often has professional qualifications but has had to resign from his/her job.
3. Spouse has free time to devote to a business since domestic help is easily available.
4. Spouse has more free time if there are no children in the family or if their children are in school.
5. Living in a foreign culture away from the normal support network of extended family and friends creates opportunities for exploring their new environment.
6. Limited support for the spouse from the expatriate's company

Expatriate assignments are often also difficult for the expatriate's company, where statistics show that 30% of all expatriate staff return early from their overseas work postings. This is due to the effects of the overseas posting on the expatriate family, putting pressure on the family members and straining family relationships, which results in increased divorce rates, and high drop-out rate from high school.

The establishment of a family business will then be explored as a proactive solution that has the potential to create positive outcomes from a traditionally difficult situation. How does one find the ingredients for a family business in the expatriate's situation? What makes a family business a solution worth considering in this case? How can coaching support this development?

The expatriate spouse becomes the emotional pillar for the family, especially during the adjustment period, where he/she has to manage adaptation and evolution in a country where sometimes they cannot even communicate due to language barriers. This situation of drastic change can be an opportunity to reflect on what the person has always wanted to do, but never did it. With coaching, it might facilitate the implementation and assertion of his or her life values in the form of a business realization.

What are the consequences of an expatriate situation for family members?

I would like to consider the expatriate situation, followed by its effects on family members.

The expatriate situation

Generally speaking, expatriates face an increase in work pressure and huge emotional challenges.

Expatriates have to live up to certain time expectations, as extra hours are expected by the company to justify their return on corporate investment. Although this is not the way it should work at the typical expatriate executive level where performance assessment should be based on results, the expatriate might feel obliged to work longer hours because of the company's investment in him in the form of his upgraded position and generous financial package. If the person does not take control, or is not conscious of this pitfall, he might start to feel overwhelmed.

The threat of work stress spilling over into family and social life is also common and real. The feeling of work overload might affect the free time after work, leading to exhaustion and stress. This is worsened by the mental stress of adjusting to a new role and a new culture/language.

Other than meeting the company's expectations for return on their investment, the expatriate faces an increased workload due to the change in the nature of work and the need for frequent travel to corporate headquarters and regional countries in their work portfolio. This interface, which is new to the expatriate, can be a source of dissatisfaction with the organizational culture and increases the chance of misunderstandings. The increased workload, when coupled with lack of organizational support and direction and the loss of the support network from their corporate head office colleagues, as well as their own extended family, will add to the stress of an overseas posting.

This feeling of isolation and excessive worrying often results in a negative psychological mood for the expatriate. This mood does not even improve with time, as most expatriates are "in transit" (2–3 years) before moving to their next posting in another country. As such, after experiencing repeated social instability, they protect themselves by not building any friendships. The emotional consequences are feelings of hopelessness, clinical depression, and addictive behaviour, such as alcoholism or shopping.

There are also negative ramifications for relationships. They might experience disappointment in relationships and discouragement at not being understood. The lack of emotional and social connections also results in loneliness.

However, the employee might overcome the challenges of his overseas job posting by remaining in a "curiosity mindset"; that is, approaching this new life's configuration as a chance for discovering and learning and enjoying the differences.

For example, Marie-Odile, a mother of three, went back to France after ten years as an expatriate's spouse. She now runs her own business selling Japanese items. She started the family business based on her experience of her stay in Japan. She learnt Japanese and received the inspiration from the Japanese way of dealing with customers. The cultural experiences gained in the places where she lived allowed her to go on to develop her own business concept successfully. The various challenges of the expatriate's life developed her sense of autonomy and adaptability. Her husband enjoyed his job posting in Japan very much, and his attitude of embracing the Japanese culture encouraged his family to do the same. Back from Japan, he has been supportive towards Marie-Odile's project in three ways: by supporting the idea enthusiastically, providing financial support as an investor, and by being more active at home and with the children—even when it meant leaving the office earlier and working from home after dinner, if necessary.

The expatriate spouse's situation

There is often a loss of the expatriate spouse's professional support network, such as colleagues, because the spouse usually has to quit his/her current job before the overseas move. The expatriate spouse also loses the support of his/her extended family and may even feel the "loss" of his/her own spouse (the expatriate) as a result of his/her long working hours and frequent travel.

In the new country, the expatriate spouse has to deal with a completely new environment, for example, unfamiliar shops, service suppliers, and government departments. The expatriate spouse also has more free time, since domestic tasks are easily and extensively "outsourced" to domestic helpers.

When the expatriate's move is restricted to husband, wife, and children, the potential of loneliness for the spouse is high: busy working husband/wife, children at school, and no members of the extended family (parents, siblings) to provide emotional support. This internal emotional pressure within the restricted system may lead to loneliness, feelings of not being heard and understood, and unexpressed sadness. The new environment may cause significant stress in adjusting to an unfamiliar culture and the challenge of learning a new language, leading to feelings of helplessness and frustration.

The expatriate spouse's level of comfort with his/her personal thoughts and emotions comes under trial, from expressing freedom from unwanted compulsions, self-acceptance, or denial. Cognitive clarity of thoughts and the ability to maintain the focus and optimism might be altered in this closed and emotional environment, leading to thoughts with scattered focus, negative feelings, and difficulty in making decisions.

Similar to the expatriate described earlier, the spouse will also experience a negative psychological mood resulting in negative ramifications for relationships.

The expatriate children situation

The expatriate children experience a loss of friends during their growing-up years. For those who have done well in school when they were in their home country and may even have the opportunity of receiving a scholarship, their potential may be curbed by their move to a new country, with their father being less present and their mother feeling lonely and isolated.

What are the opportunities for a family business startup?

Generally speaking, the following are common challenges faced in relation to setting up a family business.

- Emotional tension in the family when there is no clear line drawn between business and personal life, as family members are now business partners.
- The lack of discernment and distance between private and professional communication may lead to a feeling of not being heard and understood.
- A tendency to rely only on their own resources, due to a lack of external and supplementary resources.

Now, looking back at expatriate family models, they can present different opportunities. Following Step 2 (Form a Powerful Coalition) of Kotter's model, *Pull Together the Guiding Team*, building a family business may be an opportunity to draw the family together.

One key issue with couples is the lack of communication—"We never talk!" Building a business by drawing on each person's skills/resources in a "business-like" way, that is, decision-making guided more by data rather than emotion, may be a way to strengthen the relationship. Once a couple gets used to talking about business, it is easier to progress to other issues/topics. With the clear view that this is a way to build bridges for communication, the expatriate and the expatriate spouse can each bring different skills and contributions to the business. The expatriate working relatively long hours will not be able to help in the operations of the business, but he/she can probably contribute in a valuable way by playing a company board member-type role, that is, an independent expert providing consultancy or simply as a sounding board. Children can also be actively engaged in the family business. For example, older children can build/manage the family business website, answer email enquiries, process orders, duplicate CD/DVDs, and handle mailing. For expatriates without children, both spouses should have spare time in running the business together.

Business startup for expatriate families

Expatriates starting their own business are typically well-educated with rich job experiences. For those with newborn children or children of school age, starting a business is a way to cope with the children's schedule and to prepare for the day when the children have grown up and decide to leave home.

It is an opportunity to sit back and reflect on what they have always wanted to do, and to express their entrepreneurial streak, which is possibly something they did not dare to do before. In the expatriate context, money is usually a lesser challenge (typically, it is the same amount of family income, but now coming from only one person's salary) and, therefore, it is a good opportunity to try out being an entrepreneur. It usually takes a period of three years to develop a business to a stable stage.

As in all owner-managed business start-ups, the spouse who is managing the business is influenced by his/her spouse's life's values and perception on the degree of autonomy. It can be an integrative or disintegrative force. In the case of a supportive spouse, it helps to draw the family together, but in the case of a non-supportive spouse, it will emphasize the differences between them.

Take the case of Joelle, who has a background in advertising/marketing working in a Fortune 500 company. She had thought of a job change or embarking on entrepreneurship. After moving from France to Hong Kong with her newborn, she went back to university for a year as a means to cope with her children's schedule, and to discover Asia. She chose to study ecology and sustainable development. Then, when she moved to the UK, she realized that childcare was very expensive and, therefore, it was worthwhile to continue her studies and looking after her child. At the same time, she started developing her own website with her sister, who has technical background in website development. This experience of working with her sister has been a great way to keep contact with other family members through weekly conversations on Skype. As there was already trust established, she felt a strong desire to work with her sister and it was a natural way to move forward towards working together. After moving to Singapore, she continued developing the website as a portal for corporate social responsibility (CSR) work, also known as corporate responsibility, corporate citizenship, responsible business, sustainable responsible business (SRB), or corporate social performance, which is the deliberate inclusion of community interest into corporate decision-making, and the honouring of a triple bottom line: people, planet, profit. She started to develop a network of non-governmental organizations (NGOs) and support them in joint projects. She works on activities and projects that focus on reflection on world issues more than global corporate equity. She is always looking for ways to pursue her ideal while not neglecting family values within her professional activities. It was easy for her to set up her business in Singapore as a sole proprietorship. Her husband helps by being her business coach, and her children are very supportive about the ecological messages she advocates. Besides the success of receiving her family's love and support, her success also lies in her achievement of attaining the long-term sustainability of CSR activities (which are not primarily based on money). Her success is also largely due to her rich and varied experiences in different countries, as CSR is strongly linked to each country's local values.

Developing a business is also a way to avoid loneliness and to have a focused goal in life.

Setting up and running a business can provide a clearer vision on life's values and the possibility of increasing your work freedom and autonomy. For those who are seeking desperately for his/her own identity, developing a business can lead a person to a "survival" mode of taking care of oneself, where one is driven by emotional challenges and the search for identity. Because the values are put in place, self-assertiveness can be increased with self-interests and passion in a business startup.

For example, Marie was an IT engineer who followed her husband to Asia-Pacific for his work posting. She managed to support her family's move and adjustment to the four new countries and cultures while maintaining her own employability throughout. However, she reached her career ceiling due to her family commitments and the lack of additional corporate training. Her local employers did not invest in her training because they knew that, as an expatriate spouse, she could not be a long-term employee. She then decided to study a subject that she had an aptitude for, which is using coaching skills as a communication and team management tool. After that, she used the skills that she had learnt to launch her own practice. It was a real source of self-discovery, because by understanding herself better she was better able to attract clients, and her self-confidence gradually increased. Unfortunately, she did not receive her husband's support for her career change. This self-confidence gained through reliance on her own resources allowed her to find the strength to assert her own life and career choice. The use of YNW™ (a coaching tool that helps individuals to relearn their natural way of living their life, see www.yournaturalway.com) and self-coaching to discover her own values and strengths has also been a milestone along her path to success.

Although expatriate spouses may have the relevant skills and experience, there are fewer opportunities to work as an employee in the country of posting due to the country's local employment regulations, which may make it difficult for a foreigner to attain a work visa. It may also be difficult to find a relevant position, since potential employers know that he/she will be moving to the another country along with the next posting of their expatriate spouse.

For example, former HR Director Bertrand undertook a mid-career change in 2000, when he chose to accompany his wife on her first international assignment in the USA. In order to conciliate his own career objectives with the constraints of ongoing mobility, he set up his own HR consulting firm. From his own experience, Bertrand was convinced that accompanying spouses make up a tremendous pool of talents, which remains under-utilized because of the lack of ways for companies to identify, recruit, or assign projects to them. Therefore, he had spent the past two years setting up dualexpat.com, an intercompany career platform for expatriates. The aim of the platform is to provide expatriates and spouses with a comprehensive array of resources and opportunities to organize their mobility, manage their career, find a job, or develop their own business.

Coaching approach for expatriate family businesses

The following proposed steps in coaching expatriate family businesses are based on my own coaching practice for my expatriate family business as well as for other expatriate international businesses.

Coaching using the CSAI assessment tool can be a good starting point. The CernySmith Adjustment Index (CSAI™) is an on-line assessment tool that evaluates intercultural well-being and effectiveness for expatriates when undergoing coaching. CSAI assessments measure an Intercultural Intelligence Index (ICI). It addresses the expatriate's well-being, effectiveness, and environmental situation.

The coach must be aware of the expatriate context and be ready to strongly support the expatriate in managing emotional issues. This understanding of the emotional issues is crucial. The coach's awareness of the different grieving stages (denial, anger, bargaining, depression, and acceptance) might be useful when coaching a new expatriate.

Tremendous changes are happening in any expatriate move, and, on top of this, the switch from being a working mother to a self-employed mother/entrepreneur might involve a drastic mindset change. The coach has to be ready to support the change. It is unavoidable that members of the family will make the comparison between before and after the change in roles, thereby increasing their feelings of insecurity.

Checking with family members for their support is key for an expatriate starting a family business. The expatriate can start by asking them, and checking with them periodically to ensure alignment of thoughts and feelings.

In family businesses, there is the word "family". Therefore, it is worthwhile to embark on coaching that is based on the business itself, taking into account that it is a family business. Even thinking and reflecting on the use of profit might be a family project, too.

However, the challenge might be to persuade the expatriate spouse to invest in coaching to secure and support her/his development. Coaching on business development is then the next logical step to support in areas such as branding, marketing, and business networking, etc.

Conclusion

When an expatriate is relocated to a new country, it is a place to explore and try new possibilities that he/she might want. Entrepreneurship is a feasible work option to explore and support personal growth. Even when it is time to return to the home country, the developed competencies often proved to be very valuable for today's employment market.

In an expatriate situation, expatriates have to assert both cognitive competencies and behavioural effectiveness, such as openmindedness, respect for others, trust, tolerance, personal control, flexibility, adaptability, self-confidence, taking initiative, interest in others, and harmony in relationships.

This adventure of creating a family business in the expatriate's situation is a way to learn how to give priorities to the varied aspects of their life's journey, to keep focus, and grow on this path. It is also a means to give meaning to their own life values and eventually enrich other lives with their cross-cultural experiences and resources.

Traditionally, expatriate spouses (usually the wife) were involved in voluntary work and humanitarian activities, but now I think the trend is to develop a longer-term activity that has a deeper connection with their personal values. Since the motivation is indeed putting one's life values in place, it might be worthwhile to explore a coaching model combining these humanitarian activities with a business/family business model to create a new social entrepreneur model. It is to support the expatriate in creating a space where he/she is driven by his/her deep values and in connection with the environment (internal and external connections). This collaborative activity contributes to a responsible ecological growth (expatriate and the others), and leverages the opportunity that is given when meeting and living with people of different nationalities and cultures in this fabulous adventure.

At this stage of globalization, the expatriate situation is a perfect situation for a "butterfly effect"—a paradigm of interpersonal osmosis that can create added value and growth from diversity rather than remaining in the paradigm of difference.

> In the world of business, performance is the universal language. If you are looking to national culture for an explanation of a company's failure or success, you are missing the point! A successful business performance in America is measured the same way it is measured in Japan, Europe, China, or any other market. Quality, cost and delivery mean the same thing around the globe. Everyone counts the same way. The numbers have the same values. At the end of the day, in any time zone, value creation always will be the measure of effectiveness. [Carlos Ghosn, in Rivas-Micoud, 2005, p. 4]

Acknowledgements

Special thanks to the friends who were so keen and willing to share their experiences when asked, to David A. Lane who contacted me for this project, and to Dr M. Shams, who expressed a constant encouraging support all through my writing process.

References

Kotter, J. Step 2: form a powerful coalition. In: *Pull Together the Guiding Team.* http://www.mindtools.com/pages/article/newPPM_82. htm

Rivas-Micoud, M. (2005). *The Ghosn Factor.* Singapore: McGraw-Hill Education (Asia).

CHAPTER EIGHT

Understanding the impact of family dynamics on the family business coaching approach

V. Ramakrishnan

Introduction

F amily businesses are one of the major economy sectors in many countries. The sense of ownership drives a natural commitment, an element most "professional" businesses struggle to achieve. The problem with family business is growth. Either "the firm grows faster than the family or the family grows faster than the firm . . ."—a well-known saying.

Family businesses struggle to differentiate between the business, management, and ownership; the demands of each are different, often conflicting, and difficult to develop a package to deal with. These differences tend to diverge as successive generations move into the business, and often when one member marries into an equally affluent business family, bringing into the business portfolio a possibly different mindset and beliefs.

As with other businesses, family businesses tend to run down over time. Families prefer to play their internal politicking close to their chest as a rule, and there are numerous internal undercurrents that make free and public sharing difficult. Coaching is a powerful technique to help these businesses renew and grow.

While the dynamics of management and governance is significantly different in family owned and managed businesses, explained later in detail, the businesses may have similar goals and visions, thereby sharing the same philosophy for running a business for economic sustainability and to meet personal developmental needs.

The coach as a trusted adviser

Coaching a business executive is, essentially, developing an individual from where he or she is to where he or she wants to be. The need for coaching is based on the following assumptions.

1. The firm values the individual.
2. The inability of the concerned individual to develop self internally on their own or by using the firm's current human resource development practices is proved.
3. The individual has chosen, and committed, to make the desired changes of his or her own volition and volunteered to be coached.
4. An external facilitator or coach is recognized as being essential to help the individual in making the changes so that they become more accountable to family business functions.
5. The company is committed to facilitating the coachee's journey and is willing to "partner" the coach in the process.

In coaching a family member several, if not all, of these assumptions central to the executive coaching concept tend to fail, as explained below.

The value of the family member is seldom, if ever, in question. The firm's development planning for family members often falls short for reasons detailed later in the chapter. In many instances, the individual may not have volunteered in the true sense of the word. Given the tension arising from internal conflicts, many family members may not be willing to admit to having a shortcoming that needs correction; or worse, if coaching is seen as being fashionable, every member would want a coach of his or her choice, making the option of becoming a trusted adviser impossible. Coaching can become a fad. Last, the coach may not be easily accepted, given the need many families have for privacy.

The coach in a family business is a valued and trusted adviser. Trust is central to the family coach, has to be earned by the coach, and is never given on a platter. Coaching a family-owned business requires that coach to be seen as a partner, not as a third party contractor or a professional. It rarely is or can be an "arm's length transaction" for a reputed coach. Figure 8.1 shows the pathway to becoming a trusted adviser.

Coaching a family business requires the coach to develop the ability to walk on glass with bare feet (without screaming in pain!), given the brittle egos at stake and the potential to cause much harm if handled without due care. It is a tense, testing effort, as the cross-currents are many and masked or hidden from a stranger. As explained in the next section, family businesses value loyalty and the various factions and cohorts have their "own" loyal" employees, which has an impact on objective decision making, and hence the coaching process.

The dilemma of family business

Many families struggle with several contrasting and often conflicting issues, where a solution to one challenge rakes up a problem in another, unexpected location. Those that are overwhelmed by these dilemmas decline; those that recognize this context of these conflicting situations have the ability to turn around very fast.

The family members can maintain the status quo or drive change rapidly; both can be made to happen fast. This is the primary dilemma and sets in when there is a generational transition.

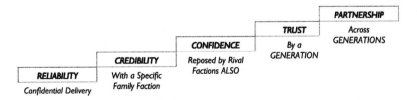

Figure 8.1.   The pathway to becoming a trusted adviser.

In a traditional family business, loyalty and not competence is often a primary virtue in rising to the top for non-family managers. This second dilemma struggles between meritocracy and loyalty; usually loyalty wins. This tendency cascades through the firm and the culture vacillates between benevolence and autocratic benevolence. People are assessed, evaluated, and promoted on the basis of their commitment to the family cause rather than objective performance. Managerial mediocrity tends to be dominant across levels within the firm, and may be even encouraged, as can be seen in numerous European old-world firms, staffed with technically competent, but managerially weak executives.

Yet, the owners would not accept a fall in overall prosperity. This contradiction has many ramifications and the coach needs to understand them. The need for success in a culture that cherishes loyalty over performance represents the third dilemma.

The final dilemma is that such mediocre teams have to keep the firm competitive, which is essential for survival. These dilemmas manifest themselves in several ways. Growth is sacrificed on the altar of upholding tradition. As a consequence, power through networks and not performance drive the organization. Coercion, in one form or the other, replaces the competitive drive. Over time, the firm is staffed with loyal under-performers. This can be a source of huge frustration for the next generation as they come into the business. Often, the older employees treat the new generation with irritating condescension. Change is slow, more so if the bulk of the ageing team have little interest in challenges as they bide their time to fade away. Growth is slowed by the lack of capital required to grow the firm and maintain a competitive edge, as such firms tend to depend on internal generation of surpluses to fund growth bolstered by banks, who tend to lend to a name rather than on a critical assessment of the business potential. Bringing in money from outside the, usually, cash-strapped business could often mean dilution of the fractured family holdings or an aggressive outsider shaking things up. This limits the firm in its ability to grow organically, from within, and, if it does it happen, it happens at a snail's pace, eroding competitiveness. Seldom would such firms approach private equity or venture capitalists, who would be aggressive in their demands for sustainable performance and intrusive in ensuring that their investments yield a fair or expected return.

The coaching process in such instances would have to develop arguments to lead the family into a one-way street of decision making. The argumentation would have to focus on detailed analysis of cause and effect, of the pros and the cons, would possibly be numerically led, with a clear assessment of the upside of doing and the downside of not doing.

The decisions can be facilitated by the coach treating this as a conflict resolution challenge.

As with other coaching approaches, the actual decision is up to the family to take; the coach can at best be a facilitator. It requires the coach to be patient, persistent, and to provide repetitive reinforcement.

Understanding the generational characteristics

Understanding the generational characteristics helps the coach develop the needed empathy. There are distinct characteristics in each generation, and this is largely true in many family businesses; for some it is overt, in others, it is subtle, and in a few, maybe covert.

The founder is the visionary, either voluntarily or involuntarily. Often the vision is vested once the business is successful. The founder has an astonishing mental map of the business and incisive intuition about what works and what does not.

The two basic elements of a first-generation business that emerge are:

1. The strengths of the owner are the weaknesses of a business.
2. The weaknesses of the owner remain the weaknesses of a business.

With the entry of the second generation in a family business, a sense of drift happens in most firms. The older employees resent the loss of the personal touch of the founder, and dislike reporting to a "kid" they brought up. The "kid", in turn, finds the condescending attitudes, which develop along with the lack of competence and drive, frustrating. The reality is that the first generation remains manipulative and critical, thus interfering with the settlement of the next generation. In such a situation, the founder retains control and drives the business, frustrating everybody, including himself. The coach would be advised to recognize these symptoms and work through the founder to streamline the succession. The coach has to work with the founder, his appointed successors, and the loyal managers to find a solution.

The third generation is usually an indulged set. The grandparents have the leisure, the stature, and the money to indulge them from birth; the second generation is either indifferent to the indulgence, or unable to prevent it. As one old man known for his strict upbringing of his children put it when caught indulging the grandchildren, ". . . I have all the fun in indulging the kids but the responsibility for making them 'well brought up children' rests with my daughter-in-law!" The third generation is protected and insulated from the reality of the family business in many ways, a situation that has profound effects on the family, the business, and the individual. This is explained in some depth later.

The third generation tends to be hands off and vulnerable to complacency. The control is diluted as the loyalists fade away and a new generation of managers takes over. Depending on the timing, this new set of managers could develop the loyalty factor with the third generation if they started alongside them or have a need to transfer their loyalties, say, to secure their positions. Both cases present challenges, as by now the third generation consists of siblings from the children of the founder; childhood, sibling, and filial rivalries tend to surface.

One family has resolved these issues simply. All family members get the same title, the same salary, and the same but very limited perks; a trust ensures the funds for education and support in a crisis. The members are free to spend their salaries as they like, after providing a contribution to running the household. This family provides no club memberships, expects all members to travel in the same class, each gets an identical car, and so on. It sounds dull and boring but does make for a smoother family working.

In yet another family, the family has created a council of third party advisers, all known to the family but considered objective well-wishers. The family members submit detailed project reports and business plans, in preparing which they get the assistance requested. The council assesses the business plans submitted by the family and decides, on a professional basis, which "project" is feasible and the level of resources that can and should be committed.

The coach has to recognize and understand the impact of these emotional realities in a family business; rational arguments and reasoning seldom work in such a situation, unless the rules of the game are clear and documented in the family charter or constitution. It takes patience, understanding, and skilful negotiation to bring about congruence in thinking within the family.

For this to happen, the coach needs to have the confidence and trust of all three generations.

Coaching the fourth generation members is easier and almost on par with that of a professional head. The needs and egos could be identical and the influence of birth order is less marked.

The family business dynamic

The difficulties and challenges inherent to a family business are large and require expert attention. The coach would be advised to understand the development of the individuals in the light of complexities of the various families' owned and managed businesses.

To facilitate the discussion and understanding of family business dynamic, a stakeholder business model is proposed to illustrate the simplicity of a professional business construct and the complexity of a family business set up. It then develops the complex constructs in family owned and managed businesses and explains step by step the maze that a family owned, professionally managed business exhibits. The section ends with a feasible "means approach".

The stakeholder business model (Figure 8.2) is simple. It separates ownership from management. There are owners, usually the promoters, or the family, or the public, or the public plus a main shareholder who provides capital but takes no part in managing or running the business day to day; there is the business management team that provides the expertise to manage the business, and there is the interface between the ownership and management. If ownership can be represented by a circle, and management by a second circle, the key issues to be resolved in managing a

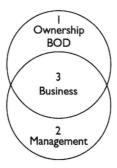

Figure 8.2. The simplicity of the stakeholder business model.

successful business are where the two circles intersect. The Venn (Venn, 1880) diagram, a set of intersecting circles, then has three distinct components.

1. Circle 1 reflects the ownership, represented by the board of directors, that has invested capital in the business and set the strategy or expectations or results the business has to deliver.
2. Circle 2 describes the management, which is responsible for execution or running the business efficiently to deliver the results that were agreed upon between the owners of capital and the managers when the resources were made available.
3. The intersection of the circles represents the business. The closer the two circles are, the greater the overlap or intersection. The overlapping area is an area where the owners and managers meet to agree on how to take the business forward and the expectations of each to develop a sound business. It defines the working relationship between the ownership and the management team. At board level, the owners set out the goals and targets and make available the resources required. At the execution level, the managers provide operational feedback, on a regular basis, of the gap between goals set, actual achievement, and the productivity of the resources. In the Anglo-Saxon world, the business represented by the area of the overlap is a distinct entity, being a "body corporate".

The shareholders appoint directors who form the board; the board sets out the vision, mission, the strategy and policy (at least it should ideally). The Chairman, usually non-executive, chairs the board meetings and is accountable for the firm's and board's performance. The CEO heads the management team, develops the deliverable objectives to meet the strategic needs, and enables his team to deliver results. Any disagreements over the running of the business, which is the interface between the board and the management, are brought to the surface in the board meetings or in the various committees the board appoints. The board has the final say and the CEO and team usually has to comply with this. There are personality conflicts and issues, but these are resolved amicably through consultation, coaching, and arbitration.

Figure 8.3 captures the relationships in a family owned and managed business (Gersick, Davis, Hampton, & Lansberg, 1997; Ward, 2004), where the ownership rests with the family and the business operation is headed by family members and the execution team, consisting of professional managers. The management responsibility, when compared to the stakeholder model, is split between the family and hired managers. Although only one additional element is added, not only are there more relationships to be managed, many are far more complex than in the stakeholder model.

The first three relationships, the ownership or board of directors, the management, the business and the relationship between the board and the management team as described in the stakeholder model, remain the same. There is one significant difference, represented by the fourth dimension and the second interface, which

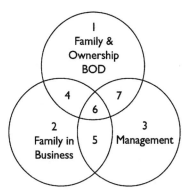

Figure 8.3. The straightforward family owned, family managed business.

needs to be managed in a family business. The board is largely family, but has non-family directors as well, and hence the decision making tends to be less objective.

The fifth relationship is when a family member is part of the management team and in the business, but is not on the board of directors, for example, when the second generation joins the firm, as a manager with an aim to becoming a director. In large families, not every family member can become a board member, while they can and do have a role in the management of the business. This duality creates tensions between siblings, as detailed earlier.

The sixth aspect of being a family member is when the person has all three roles to play, as an owner, a director, and a business manager, the area enclosed by the boundaries of the three circles. Such situations make the person virtually above the normal rules of the game and the blurred boundaries between the roles can cause confusion both to the person and to the organization. Clear boundaries of behaviour have to be drawn up and accepted; the sooner such conflicting roles are eliminated, the better it is for the firm.

The last situation is when a non-family member is appointed as a director. Given that management of family businesses tend to be staffed with timeservers, this elevation can cause a lot of conflicts among the less loyals who were not made "director". Further, the promotee seldom is willing to learn the difference between a director and a manager, and this leads to what is called the Executive Board (Garratt, 2003a, pp. 40–41) being known as the "Rubber Stamp" board.

In family owned and managed businesses, setting strategy is difficult, as each family member who does not work in the firm has other ideas (see Figure 8.4). In a recent instance, the fifth generation member of a long and established Asian firm, well settled professionally in the USA, advised his uncle, the group Chairman, to scuttle the forty million dollar expansion and split the cash! Furthermore, not all family members sit on the board, although the tendency is to assign one seat to each family member—and that is where the trouble starts. Each member intends to put forward their opinions, which usually are rejected by another member for sheer pleasure only, without understanding the benefits it may bring to the overall business functions and output.

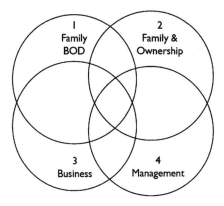

Figure 8.4. The complex family owned, professionally managed firm.

The solutions to this are discussed separately in the section entitled " The need for a family constitution", which is emerging as the most plausible solution to a sustainable progress of a family business in the global world. It is also proving to be effective, in my experience, as it combines the inherent commitment of the founder with the consummate managerial skills of the professional. Almost all recent successes in the past two decades—Microsoft, Google, eBay, Apple—reflect this architecture: a strong founder driving the direction the business has to take, and a competent leadership team of professionals managing the business efficiently.

The contrast between family firms and professionally managed firms

It is important to understand the key differences between the way a professionally managed firm, typified by a multi-national corporation, or MNC, is managed and governed and the manner in which family businesses are managed and governed. This comparison is essential to explain the coaching process for a complex family owned and professionally managed firm. The main points covering the differences between the main business elements are represented in Table 8.1.

In a family business where strategies and decision making is usually *ad hoc*, such structured systems are scoffed at or vitiated.

Table 8.1.   Structural representation of non-family and family businesses.

Key business elements	Non-family business	Family business
Strategy	Planned	Flexible
Structure	Complex	Hierarchical
Systems	Sophisticated	Minimal
Policy	Clear do's and don'ts	Trivial
People	Performance driven	Loyalty critical
Processes	Integrity vital	Ignored or subverted
Management	Over managed	Under managed
Governance	Under governed	Over governed

Multi-national corporations develop and deploy sophisticated systems to ensure that communication required to deliver complex strategies is comprehensive and can compete to support decision making. Family businesses may like to be "certified" for business systems like ISO etc., but seldom adhere to the spirit and discipline these qualifications require. A coach can pick this up with a cursory audit.

MNCs are driven by policy; once set by the board they are the law, and violation has strong consequences. In a family business, the family is the law and, hence, there is little need for a policy. People are valued for their loyalty and, therefore, processes in family businesses tend to be sloppy at best and usually ignored. As a consequence, family businesses tend to be under managed and over governed; in contrast, professionally run businesses tend to be over managed and under governed, for example, by applying unified rules across the global operation, some of which may not have the same relevance globally as they do in a local context. Such rules make management easy but governance difficult.

A coach who has come through the MNC ranks would find such chaos horrifying. The question that needs to be asked and answered is, "How is that these family businesses still survive and thrive?" And the fact is, many do, simply because the commitment of the family member and employees is naturally driven, unlike in an MNC, where people have to be motivated with pay for performance and town hall meetings to stay committed. It is unbelievable but true how the loyal dedicate themselves to a family cause.

The good practice in coaching in this situation is to find a platform between the successful MNC model and the non-systematized family business. This is shown in Table 8.2, which is self-explanatory. A family business provides an opportunity to be both well managed and well directed more conveniently than a professional firm because exceptions can be flagged, escalated, and resolved quickly, without undue political interference.

The coach should stress the benefits of group thinking, sharing, and a practical approach to achieving results in a family business context. The difficult areas are getting the rank and file into an achievement mode, and to get systems thinking inculcated

A simple example: many firms require that every employee's car is checked by the security staff on leaving the premises. How many family members would suffer this indignity? And in one instance, a clever administration staff member takes his bag containing critical business information and leaves the premises deep in discussion with the owner in the latter's car, escaping a check!

These are generic descriptors and vary according to the family and business types. The coach can be aware of these pitfalls. Solutions have to be engineered around the specific factors influencing the business. If the rules of engagement (a family charter or constitution) are written up, it makes system adherence and process integrity better. This is best embodied in a "family constitution".

If a constitution has to be written, it is best written by the first, and, if not feasible, the second generation of leaders. The third-generation relationships are so complex and fraught that it is a

Table 8.2. Systematic and planned family business.

Key business elements	Non-family business	Family business
Strategy	Planned	Flexible thinking-structured planning
Structure	Complex	Adaptive
Systems	Sophisticated	Practical
Policy	Clear do's and don'ts	Productivity driven
People	Performance driven	Achievement orientated
Processes	Integrity vital	Preserved
Management	Over managed	Well managed
Governance	Under governed	Well governed

Herculean task to write up on. Each relationship must be recognized, the roles clarified, the do's and don'ts listed. It is also important to define the escalation, arbitration, and dispute resolution mechanism. Some families keep this to the bare bones and use mentors or advisers to resolve conflicts. In many families, the wealth is allocated, when an elder dies intestate, by such informal arbitration mechanisms as asking an elder to come up with a fair resolution.

Spelling out with clarity the separation between the family, the ownership, the business, and the management is a complex task; implementing it is a huge challenge both in terms of governance and emotions. The challenge often arises as the third and subsequent generations take charge. An example of how foresight can protect reputation follows.

The constitution of one family, with much foresight, recognized the need for the sense of identity that the family name carried as a brand; this necessitated the need to ensure prudence in its use to protect a reputation established over a century in business. Hence, a significant element in the charter was the management of the brand and logo and how their availability and use would devolve from the holding or parent company to the more recent avatars. The family had several main lines of business, each originally pioneered by the first- and second-generation founders and nurtured by the third generation. Each line of business was handed over to a fourth generation family member and the conditions for use of the logo and brand were as shown below:

1. Each line of business would use the same logo and font but with different colour schemes. This ensured that each business has a distinct identity, but its group affiliation was clear and unambiguous. This set out the family-business nexus clearly.
2. The logo was usable only if a family member was the head of the business. This helped cement family control over management. It was necessary because many of the firms went public and the family share-holdings were diluted.
3. The logo was usable provided the business paid a tiny fraction of its revenue as a fee for the right to use the brand name and logo. This money added to the wealth and went into a trust

used for philanthropy and to meet the needs of the family members for education, medical care, and retirement. This sum was independent of any royalties from patents held by the trust or from dividends. Management had no say in the amount or validity of the payment. It was a charge of the business and expensed before tax.

4.   The family member had to sign a code of ethics. Any violation could lead to a withdrawal of the rights to use the brand name and logo. This ensured that management was forced to keep its nose clean, establishing the need to protect reputation.

Some years after the roll-out, one firm in the family group had the right to use the brand and logo withdrawn when it violated key regulatory guidelines and ran afoul of the regulatory statutes. The clarity in the charter, emotional as the decision was, helped the family steer clear of a disastrous situation, and the trust did help bail out the member concerned. The family board orchestrated the decision and ensured its reputation remained intact.

The coach cannot and should not attempt to devise all the mechanisms required to be in a constitution: legal, tax, company law, trust and anti-trust laws are all involved and require specific expertise and input. The coach can, and should, however, help the family bring all these elements together to the acceptance, if not satisfaction, of all the family members. These descriptions are provided as insights, which can help a coach to intervene and apply appropriate coaching approaches to build consensus.

The need for a family constitution

Family businesses have a distinct set of rules by which they are governed. These are not extrapolations of a professionally owned and run business. The principles and ethics that are common to non-family businesses, of course, are relevant and valid in a family business, but should be handled with care.

The constitution enumerates the rules that spell out, in principle and substance, how engagement *and* disengagement has to work. It helps to have clear ethical guidelines and value systems spelt out. Defining a complete and comprehensive constitution or charter is beyond the scope of a typical coach and is a separate exercise in itself, requiring specialist and knowledgeable help from legal experts. Suffice it to say that such framed rules are essential for the success and growth of family businesses. One such instance is explained in broad terms.

Many family businesses start with cross holdings in the formative years. This is unavoidable, as resources are limited and the trust between the first generation is generally good, if not implicit. Families that have anticipated the stresses that succeeding generations will probably face as a result of these cross holdings and written up a constitution to ensure a smooth transfer and/or sharing, have fared well. Families into the second generation who have ignored framing a working set of rules to govern the family are in deep distress. The crux of this constitution is that inherited wealth has to be nurtured and enhanced for ensuing generations; it cannot be eroded. Income earned independent of the wealth has to bolster the inherited wealth *and* the balance can be dispensed with by the family member concerned. Many in the third generation have successfully branched out into unrelated businesses with seed capital from the family wealth while retaining a stake in the family business. Yet others of the third generation have stayed close to the knitting and are intent on growing and nurturing the inherited business.

This family spent millions to pay capital gains and other taxes to untangle the cross holdings to give each of the second generation a clear line of sight and control over the business, as was detailed in their charter. The intent was to split the wealth to provide independent control. The cousins could hold shares in each other's firms and sit on each other's boards, but by invitation only; the wealth was clearly divided to be independent of any cross holding, at a considerable cost, by the founding fathers. The third and fourth generation are now entering the business and, in once instance, the fifth is being readied to join. Each of the businesses has grown manifold; the businesses have had their cycles, but the family unity remains. This has ensured that the third and fourth generations are inheriting flourishing businesses but no central pool of wealth, as this was split up in the separation of wealth from ownership. It is an edifying sight to see the younger generation seek council from the elders in this family.

In a contrasting situation, the last of the first generation, sadly with rather playful adult children, has steadfastly refused to consider laying out the rules of behaviour. His concern has been that the discipline of such a system would cripple his wayward sons. The family uses the same brand name for all its businesses and locations. The third generation is in the business and immensely frustrated at the rank bad governance of the uncles. Each family member has "taken over" a specific outlet and lives off its earnings; the less successful ones hit the family pot for indulging their extravagance. Yet others have divorced themselves from the family brand and are creating their own identities. The individuals have prospered; the family has lost it, and is unlikely to benefit from coaching because the divisions and distrust are so deep now, all in the space of three years! It is heartening, however, that several of the second and third generation are seeking the services of a coach to streamline the businesses they have taken control of!

The need for renewal of a business

Every business has to renew or refresh its ability to provide a product or service relevant to the emerging market. The renewal can be organic or driven by acquiring external businesses. Organic renewal appears to be the preferred route for family business and coaching can be of immense assistance in making such decisions.

Some definitions to set the context

Organic renewal is a process where a business leverages its inherent competencies to grow the business. Organic growth contrasts with growth through mergers and or acquisitions. Organic growth could be enlarging the geographic footprint of a business, going into upstream or downstream products that will expand the mother business, or spinning off specific elements of the parent to set it on its own growth path.

Organic growth can come with and through acquisitions, joint ventures where the parent firm remains the dominant partner but not in deals where it becomes a minority.

Organic growth, while possibly slower, ensures that the family remains in control. Families do not like to lose control and, hence, are prudent in their borrowings. Once a certain degree of affluence is reached and there is sufficient wealth and income streams, families tend to save and invest. Bankers know them and trust them.

Organic growth requires that the business should earn the cash required to grow the footprint, the product offering, businesses to invest in or buy into.

Family businesses tend to shy away from mergers, as they believe it will lead to a loss of control over the business and the brand. In a recent discussion, one family board member, when evaluating a joint venture where both parties would hold equal stakes with anti-dilution rights, termed it a creeping acquisition! When pressed on why he thought so his answer was brief, though not to the point: "That is my opinion and I will not change it."

An experienced coach can guide the family through the process, help them evaluate the pros and the cons objectively, and help create a consensus among the various factions. The coach can be a good arbitrator, but not a judge.

Better still if the coach can help set up a constitution where the rules that govern a merger or joint venture or acquisition can be set out. It helps the coach to have clarity on the key, universal governance principles involved.

The focused coaching approach: the three dimensions of governance

Family businesses, through their inherent lack of clarity, need a strong set of governing principles. A coach can help set the framework for good governance, the three pillars of which are accountability, transparency, and integrity. While the general principles are simple enough, each family governance framework has to be tailored to the needs on the ground. The need is defined by the age of the business, the size of the family, the nature and type of cross holdings, the formal and informal rules of behaviour that have evolved, the number of families and family members that own the firms, the number in the management, the relation between the various siblings, the role of the elders, and the way the family has managed past transitions and upheavals. As a rule, family members dislike accountability, want the managers to have integrity, and value transparency selectively.

Coaching family members is about inculcating the principles of governance, which are universal. The three points mentioned below, the three dimensions of governance, which help to draw a focused coaching approach, are:

1. How the board runs (or should run) and how it works, the board processes for setting strategy, assessing risk, understanding the meta scenarios, building leadership depth, succession planning, etc.
2. How to improve the ability of the firm to compete and how to ensure that resources such as assets, capital, cash, people, knowledge, family ties and networks can be leveraged productively. Succession planning and structuring businesses are central in this role.
3. How to translate the strategy to deliver profitable growth, which is about developing key result areas (KRAs) and setting key performance indicators (KPIs). This helps set up the "governance or directoral dashboards" (Garratt, 2003b) a framework for performance measurement required to ensure quality execution, which is vital for success.

The coach has to leverage these basic principles into principles, specific constructs, and operating rules to direct the energies of the constituent members to make the business potentially successful. The solution should ensure renewal from within the family, a process internal to the family exclusively. If all fails, external assistance may be essential and that, too, needs a framework for hiring, working, and rewarding the hired professional while protecting and growing the family wealth.

Further study areas and conclusion

The intent has been to share experiences on the dynamic nature of family businesses. Much of it is based on observation, experience, and engagement; a formal academic basis is well worth the effort considering that over 90% of wealth in the world is generated (and large portions possibly destroyed) by family owned businesses. It is clear that more detailing of examples and a chapter on the constitution *per se* would be welcome additions; space and scope of the chapter limit this.

Many of the behaviours described seemed to be common across cultures, locations, and size. These are worth understanding from the behavioural, managerial, and psychological perspectives.

Successful coaching entails gaining unconditional trust and helping family members to develop an objective and focused goal to achieve in a family business context. Understanding the dynamics of a family relationship, as distinct from that of a professionally owned and run organization, is vital to gaining trust and establishing good governance. Once gained, the trust can help the normal coaching process, which can be enhanced with extra coaching aids, such as family constitution and internal family dynamic framework, along with a clear understanding of contextual factors in which a family business operates.

Acknowledgement

I would like to acknowledge the encouragement from Professor David A. Lane to share my experiences and insights in coaching families and to Professor Manfusa Shams for her persistent efforts and patience to editing my chapter from a non-academic to a reasonably scholarly and convincingly pragmatic chapter.

References

Garratt, B. (2003a). *The Fish Rots from The Head*. London: Profile Books.
Garratt, B. (2003b). Directoral dashboards: the new board metrics. In: *Thin on Top: Why Corporate Governance Matters and How To Measure and Improve Board Performance* (pp. 142–168). London: Nicholas Brealey.
Gersick, K. E., Davis, J. A., Hampton, M. M., & Lansberg, I. (1997). *Generation to Generation: Life Cycles of the Family Business* (Chapters 1–3). Boston, MA: Harvard Business School Press.

Venn, J. (1880). On the diagrammatic and mechanical representations of propositions and reasonings. *Dublin Philosophical Magazine and Journal of Science, Series 5, 9*(59): 1–18.

Ward, J. L. (2004). The owner-managed business. In: *Perpetuating the Family Business: 50 Lessons Learned from Long Lasting, Successful Families in Business* (pp. 43–65). Basingstoke: Palgrave Macmillan.

CHAPTER NINE

Conclusions and future directions

Manfusa Shams

With increasing competition in the global economy market, a business set up within a family context appears to be the most desirable option for getting optimum levels of achievement in the economic sector around the world. The statistical evidence of 65–80% of all businesses in the world being family business (*Nation*, 2004), with 80% of family businesses from the USA and Europe (Flintoff, 2002) is in support of this accessible option for economy growth. The present estimate of 75% of all businesses in the UK (Jackson & Shams, 2006) being family businesses is supporting this trend.

Family business has been characterized as a unique economic organization for the pattern of ownership, governance, management, and succession, influencing the organization's goals, strategies, structure, and the functional strategies designed to transfer succession to the next generation (Chua, Chrisman, & Sharma, 1999).

Family businesses function around families; families, in turn, determine the nature and extent of business. With diverse family systems in different cultures, we must discuss the implications of diverse coaching approaches for family businesses within and beyond a particular cultural context.

Birley (2001) has cautioned about the misleading attempt to generalize family business as a homogenous group indicating distinctive differences in terms of attitudes towards family business among various countries, for example, Indian, Japanese, and Americans consider their businesses as family businesses, however, people from Poland and Italy have different attitudes, implying three possible explanations for such differential attitudes towards family business: "the family in", "the family out", and the "family-business jugglers" attitudes. The "family in" attitude asserts the definite entry of family members into the business and taking succession, while the "family out" and "family-business jugglers" are indecisive in terms of entry into the family business. Family business coaching, therefore, needs to incorporate both cognitive and behavioural aspects of families within a business environment so that a tailor-made coaching approach is in place for practitioners and coaches.

The literature in coaching is increasingly showing the use of diverse approaches and methods to explicate coaching, yet a clear line of research base is lacking (Grant, 2003). The tendency to focus on the "return in investment" in coaching fails to consider the subjective experience of the coaches (Leedham, 2005), group dynamics in family business, and a family-centred approach to show the importance and application of this approach to family business coaching.

If a business is carried on using a family-centred approach, then we must consider the possibility of developing a family-centred coaching approach. Localized knowledge has a significant influence on the way a business operates and functions (Shams, 2006), hence businesses originating from a local context must have such influences on business progress and for employee performance. The psychological practice in coaching must consider the context in which a coaching practice was developed (Shams, 2011).

We need to develop a family-centred coaching approach with business coaches, and practitioners, in consultation with the family business owners. This book aims to showcase such endeavours from some leading practitioners and international family business coaches. With this vision in mind, our authors have set out to capture essential elements in family business coaching with the aim of proposing and developing coaching approaches and techniques for application to local and international family businesses around the world.

I am going to present a summary of major issues arising from the discussion in each chapter to generate further interest, and to draw attention to family businesses and encourage coaches to develop family-centred approaches and techniques. The aim is also to show how the essential theme arising from a summary of these chapters is also being served by the working coaching model for family business in Chapter Two ('Recent developments . . .').

Key issues

The key issues for coaching family business are related to different dynamic functions of a family, for example, interpersonal communication, differential attitudes among generations, family values and goals, leadership pattern, and support system/network. The major issues are depicted in Figure 9.1.

The coaching practice here is dictated by the functional elements of a family. For example, if there is a lack of trust and communication in a family, then the coaching session must include family members' communication and interpersonal relationship issues.

The challenging question in this context is, what comes first in the coaching approach for a family business—family or business?

Indeed, many family businesses give priority to business growth rather than family, with the role of non-family members being predominant in these cases, whereas, in others, families are given paramount importance and businesses functions around families. Therefore, any problem with family functions brings

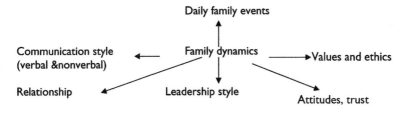

Figure 9.1. Essential elements in family dynamics.

inevitable business problems and may even hamper progress and further growth. This is depicted eloquently in Chapter Eight.

The discussions in all chapters have indeed confirmed the central role of family functions to determine business functions, irrespective of business types and location of the family business. In addition, any anomalies in family functions causing disturbances in family business and leading to decreasing levels of quality performance have been highlighted with the help of case studies from business coaches in all chapters. This leads to the assertion that family coaching should be embedded within family business coaching. Excluding family coaching from business coaching would provide only an incomplete and partial coaching practice for the family business. This also indicates the importance of applying appropriate family coaching techniques, which appear to be grounded in psychometric tools with a focus on family therapy and counselling. The increasing importance of a family constitution/charter as a compass for the family business, and organic renewal of family business through generational transmission of business capabilities are, nevertheless, demanding attention in order to develop these issues further for the sustainable growth of a family business, as is presented in Figure 9.2.

The key issues discussed in the practitioners' and professionals' chapters focus on developing theoretical frameworks and models for application to coaching practice. The discussion in this section is drawn from personal coaching experiences as well as deep understanding of, and knowledge about, family business coaching practice for local and international businesses in different locations around the world. The reliability and validity of these models are supported by relevant case studies. The emphasis is on the coachee-

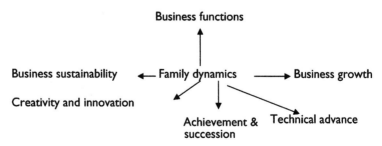

Figure 9.2.   Positioning family dynamics in the context of a family business.

centred/focused approach in coaching, thereby promoting self-awareness and growth in psychological capabilities from a coachee perspective. An integrative approach and a universal framework for coaching family businesses across cultures have been put forward in the practitioner's portfolio. The roles of cognitive–behavioural and solution-focused approaches in family business coaching have been reaffirmed in these chapters, and suggestions have been made to make further developments in equipping family business coaching with appropriate psychological models, approaches, and techniques.

The central issue running through all chapters is the reliance on family dynamics to ensure an effective coaching practice for a family business. Family is the core in a family business; as such, the starting point in a coaching is to develop trust with family members to ensure effective outcomes through the use of good family-focused coaching techniques. Family is a major marker of a family business and plays a powerful role in regulating business functions and in reaching the target goal for a family business. Unlike any other coaching, the coaching for a family business shows a need for two-tier coaching approaches and techniques, in which dual partnerships between a family and the family business can be ensured. The relationship between a family and the business is uni-directional and linear: for example, if a family is dysfunctional then this will lead to a failure in business functions; however, if a business fails then this is unlikely to lead to a dysfunctional family. The process in a family business is cyclical, as depicted in Figure 9.3, and as such, family dynamics are determining business functions, business functions are guided by family constitutions, family constitutions are aids in reaching business goals and getting business outcomes, and business outcomes/achievements are influencing family dynamics.

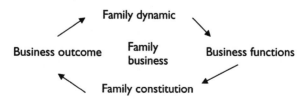

Figure 9.3. Cyclical processes in a family business.

To summarize, the major issues indicate the complexity of understanding coaching concepts, particularly in relation to family business coaching. The coaching practice for a family business is a challenging task because of possible dual-coaching in one business context: as such, the design of a coaching approach gives rise to the tension of addressing two related coaching practices under one setting/coaching context. The dramatic events in a family's life can be captured with a coaching technique, which will then facilitate coaching for the family business. This can be accomplished with the help of a spatial diagrammatic relationship framework (Shams & Lane, 2008), known as a genogram, and relationship dynamics in an ecological context, called an ecomap. A genogram is a tool for gathering data about a family's structural and process elements and relationships across generations, providing a map of the family system and relationships, and offering an educational framework for exploring family system concepts with the families as part of the assessment and intervention phases of the consultation (Brown, 1999). A genogram is expected to offer a prospective practical tool for mapping, exploring, and understanding both the structural and process elements of a family system. It is a guide to entering the family business world and a companion in the tracing of family structure, communication, and the emotional aspects of family relationship. An ecomap is a flow diagram that maps family and community systems' process over time (Hartman, 1979). It draws attention to the ecological system, which includes family and the total environment. An ecomap is built on a genogram and the functional relation is similar to a solar system: thus, a family genogram is placed in the position of the sun, at the centre, and other important people and institutions in their life space are depicted by circles around the centre, like planets around the sun. The key features in these two practical models are:

- symbolic representation of family structure and process;
- symbolic representation of a family business's position in the community;
- the ecology of family business;
- practical symbolic coaching tools for a family business.

Good practice in family business coaching should be extended to include innovative, dynamic action models (genogram and ecomap) with a focus on developing enhanced, specialized coaching skills. In addition, a family system dynamics framework can help to develop and refine professional and practical skills in coaching family businesses. There are also few other appropriate symbolic representations (Palmer, 2009) in family business coaching practice, indicating the value and applicability of symbolic models in family business coaching.

The major issues discussed and extrapolated from the rich arguments in each chapter are presented in schematic diagrams below. The aim is to help our readers identify the developmental needs of these critical and major issues in family business coaching. It also aims to capture the essential partnership between coaches and family businesses through an appropriate coaching practice, which will appreciate and value family dynamics in coaching.

Conclusion

Family business coaching will benefit from ongoing discussions on various related areas in coaching psychology, especially in showing how coaching is different yet similar to many related concepts and practices. In Chapter One ('Key issues in family business coaching'), the author argues for a careful consideration of the usage of synonymous psychological constructs and the importance of highlighting overlapping issues in coaching psychology for advancing knowledge in this area. The future of family business coaching warrants systematic exploration of conceptual development, as well as empirical research to provide evidence to support theoretical development. The good practice of family business coaching requires a clear understanding of the subject matter and related ethical issues.

Family business coaching is a complex area, as it involves dual coaching of family and family business. Hence, the dilemma is: what comes first? How should the coaching practice be developed? How might we be sure that the inseparable parts of family and family business are addressed appropriately in the same coaching practice? This warrants ongoing research and documentation of coaches' and practitioners' unique and deep coaching experiences, including suggestions on coaching tools for family businesses. Family business coaching will eventually take a central position in coaching psychology, and will be able to serve the needs of family businesses to arrive at sustainable growth, and to help families grow in the economic areas of society.

References

Birley, S. (2001). Owner-manager attitudes to family and business issues: a 16th century study. *Entrepreneurship: Theory and Practice*: 63–76.

Brown, M. (1999). Bowen family systems theory and practice: illustration and critique. *A. N. Z. J. Fam. Ther.*, 20(2): 94–103.

Chua, J. H., Chrisman, J. J., & Sharma, P. (1999). Defining the family business by behaviour. *Entrepreneurship: Theory and Practice, 23*(4): 19–39.

Flintoff, J. P. (2002). Managing to keep the family happy. *Financial Times*, 21 August, and *Behaviour and Research, 10*(1/2): 34–48.

Grant, A. M. (2003). The impact of life coaching on goal attainment, metacognition and mental health. *Social Behaviour and Personality, 31*(3): 253–264.

Hartman, A. (1979). *Finding Families: An Ecological Approach to Family Assessment in Adoption*. Beverly Hills: Sage.

Jackson, P., & Shams, M. (2006). *Developments in Work and Organizational Psychology: Implications for International Business*. The Netherlands: Elsevier.

Leedham, M. (2005). The coaching scorecard: a holistic approach to evaluating the benefits of business coaching. *International Journal of Evidence-based Coaching and Mentoring, 3*(2): 30–44.

Nation (2004). Baker and McKenzie: unique needs of family firms. *Nation, The Thailand*, 26 July.

Palmer, S. (2009). Deserted island technique: demonstrating the difference between musturbatory and preferential beliefs in cognitive behavioural and rational coaching. *The Coaching Psychologist, 5*(2): 127–129.

Shams, M. (2006). Approaches in business coaching: exploring context-specific and cultural issues. In: P. Jackson & M. Shams (Eds.), *Developments in Work and Organizational Psychology: Implications for International Business* (pp. 229–244). The Netherlands: Elsevier.

Shams, M. (2011). Developing coaching skills for international businesses: transferable and culturally appropriate. *The Special Group in Coaching Psychology Workshop* (webinar), 8 March 2011, UK.

Shams, M., & Lane, D. (2008). Development of business coaching using a family-centred approach. Workshop for the Special Group in Coaching Psychology, The British Psychological Society.

INDEX